J. M. SMITH

Other Books by ERNEST DIMNET:

IN FRENCH:

LES SOEURS BRONTË

(Paris, Bloud, 1910.) Translated into English. (London, Jonathan Cape, 1927; New York, Harcourt Brace & Co., 1928.)

FIGURES DE MOINES

(Paris, Perrin, 1908.) Crowned by the French Academy.

LA PENSÉE CATHOLIQUE EN ANGLETERRE

(Paris, Lecoffre, 1905.) Out of print.

IN ENGLISH:

THE ART OF THINKING

(Simon and Schuster, 1929.)

FROM A PARIS BALCONY

(London, Grant Richards, 1924.)

FRENCH GRAMMAR MADE CLEAR

(London, Routledge; New York, Funk & Wagnalls, 1924.)

FRANCE, HER ALLIES AND HER PROBLEMS

Six Lectures at the Institute of Politics, Williamstown, Mass.

HAS FRANCE GAINED ANYTHING BY THE WAR?

Eight Lectures at the Lowell Institute, Boston, Mass.

THE TENDENCIES OF FRENCH THOUGHT

(Oxford University Press, 1915.)

THE MARCH TO TIMBUCTOO

(By Joffre.) Translation and Preface. (London, Chatto & Windus, 1915.)

FRANCE HERSELF AGAIN

(London, Chatto & Windus, 1914; New York, Putnam, 1914.)

PAUL BOURGET: AN ESSAY IN LITERARY BIOGRAPHY

(London, Constable, 1912.)

IN LATIN:

LATINE DE ROMANIS

(Paris, de Gigord, 1924.)

Photograph by Sherrill Schell

Ernest Dimnet

Ernest Dimnet

WHAT WE LIVE BY

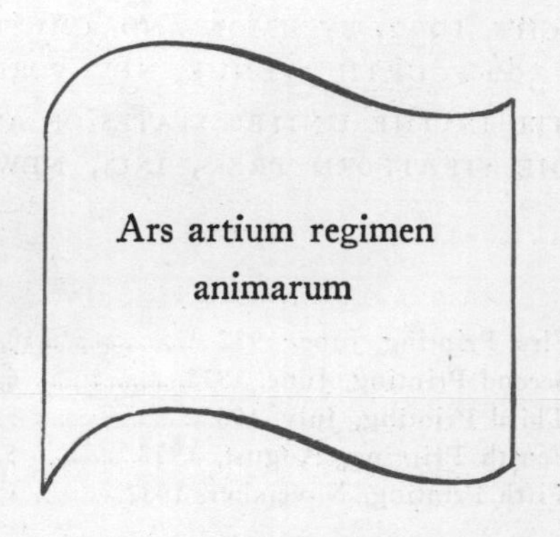
Ars artium regimen animarum

SIMON AND SCHUSTER
NEW YORK

386 FOURTH AVENUE, NEW YORK
PRINTED IN THE UNITED STATES OF AMERICA
BY THE STRATFORD PRESS, INC., NEW YORK

Printing	Copies
First Printing, June, 1932	10,000
Second Printing, June, 1932	6,000
Third Printing, July, 1932	5,000
Fourth Printing, August, 1932	5,000
Fifth Printing, November, 1932	5,000
Total	31,000

CONTENTS

CONTENTS

CONTENTS

CONTENTS

PART THREE

BONUM—BEAUTY IN LIFE

CONTENTS

CONTENTS

CONTENTS

PREFACE

THERE would be more affectation than sincerity in pretending that nothing exceptional has happened to me during the past four years. Even if I did not mention the welcome given to my last book, my readers would not believe that I was not thinking of it as I began another. Since the spring of 1929 I have received from unknown friends in America several hundred letters which could not but strengthen the bonds between that country and myself. Those bonds, that peculiar relationship I have to recognize. But a public acknowledgment of this kind is not so easy as it seems. Americans are harder to please than they imagine. They complain when the "patronizing foreigner" is too irritating, but when the foreigner, instead of being superior, feels in full sympathy with much that is specifically American and expresses this sympathy, sometimes people suspect either his intelligence or the purity of his intentions, and *he* is patronized. Clichés, you say; those critics write quickly, have to write quickly, and they fall naturally into one of two rhythms: rebelling or chaffing. Quite so; rhythms are to blame, but rhythms are like habits, sometimes pleasant, sometimes the reverse. It is therefore with a little apprehension that I feel in duty bound to say that there is something warmer at present in my relations with the American public than there was four years ago and I am deeply grateful that it is so.

Not all the letters that I received were unreservedly complimentary. In many of them a criticism was veiled under the question: "Why did you give so much space to the intellect and so little to the soul?" Often this nuance was delicately expressed: "Now you have advised us about thinking tell us how we should live."

Of course, there was under the apparent and inevitable intellectualism of *The Art of Thinking* something which could not be called purely intellectual: the conviction that the nobler the life, the higher the thinking must be. But I gradually realized that what many readers of that book had appreciated the most was suggested by it rather than actually in it. The fascination of a life above the ordinary, the retirement into one's better self, had been the poles of attraction for my correspondents, and I could see both at work in their letters.

All this meant writing another book, which fortunately had been more than once in my mind.

We are all conscious of living our moral life, as it were in a two-storied house. Downstairs goes on what has too evident a claim to the painful label: ordinary. Upstairs we have a different outlook and associate with better company. Not that our everyday routine should be called ordinary. Donatello was not ordinary when he walked home from market carrying his weekly provision of eggs in his apron. Otherwise his Florentine contemporaries would not have gazed at those eggs with so much interest. When Emily Brontë kept a German book open on the window-sill where she was preparing to beat the carpets she was not saved from being ordinary by the German book, but by the thoughts which would go on as she went through the dusty process. Does not Saint Augustine say that many people who seem to be outside the Church are actually in it and conversely? In the same way the thoughts which ought to be active in the drawing-room are sometimes relegated to the kitchen while Madame on her *chaise-longue* follows pretty trivial mental images. There is no truer saying than that intention is the soul of action.

We know perfectly well when and how we can be upstairs and when and how we linger downstairs. But it would be well if we would, every few days, look at some such chart as the following, drawn up, of course, by ourselves:

Downstairs	Upstairs
narrow ideas	silence
petty sentiments	solitude
small grievances	choosing one's company
small triumphs	indifference to trifles
egoism	reading with a purpose
conceit	studying great issues
self-praise	moral viewpoint in politics
gossip	recreation in art
flattery	intelligent travel
flirtations	love of nature
time-killing	good music
useless travelling	best plays
frivolous week-ends	best books
continuous radio	devotion to an idea
tyrannical business	devotion to a cause
tyrannical details	self-reform for a cause
vanity	

Downstairs	Upstairs
climbing	kindness
intriguing	forgiveness
pretence	patience
posing	real religion

Such a chart, referring to one's own—not to other people's—possibilities, would tell us at a glance on what storey we happen to be. We can delude ourselves, of course: tired people—tired by overwork, by age or by success—easily think they have a right to lazing downstairs. On the other hand, over-sensitive people, accustomed by frequent self-defence to thinking themselves always in the right, will entertain no doubts that their whole life is spent upstairs. However, the attraction of nobility is so strong that it leaves no room for real insincerity. In some way or another we want to be aristocrats; we have no doubt in our heart of hearts that true felicity is inseparable from distinction, and when we enjoy cheap good times downstairs we never cease to be aware that there could be a different kind of happiness upstairs. But what makes distinction? The answer is written large around us. Look at the people whom your better judgment and higher aspirations rightly cause you to envy, you will find that they are distinguished in three ways: the superiority of their thoughts, their enjoyment of beauty, or their effort to raise themselves and others to a higher moral level. The magic spell which leads the world belongs to thinkers, to artists, to moralists and religionists. And what makes such people great also makes them enviable and happy. Whatever their outward circumstances may be, we know that their interior life can never be a failure. Michelangelo was ill-treated by the world, but only a man able to rise above disappointment could have written the sonnets to Vittoria Colonna. Read the letters, recently published, which poor Gauguin wrote from Tahiti; they are an endless wailing, sometimes a positive cursing of destiny. But when, at intervals, the painter speaks of his art, of some new inspiration which possesses him, instantly the dark page becomes illuminated by delight. We never hesitate about those things. A sure instinct guides us because there are in us two tendencies which seem inseparable and irrepressible: the longing to live happy and the dread of *DYING ORDINARY*.

The present book is an effort to help and direct those tendencies in us. An ambitious enterprise? Nobody knows it better than I do. *Ars artium regimen animarum.* "The Art of Arts is the guidance of the soul." Spiritual writers, even in great repute, have repeated this a hundred times, harping on the danger of misunderstanding or being misunderstood, of creating illusions or developing dangerous complexes. And I am not a spiritual writer, I have no aptitude for ever becoming one, and I am conscious of my own deficiencies to the extent of imagining they must be as hateful to others as they are to me.

However, this is not a spiritual book. It is merely a quest of what the True, the Beautiful and the Good can mean to us, the kind of meditation which anybody would embark upon in the hope of improving his moral chances. A French Swedenborgian of the eighteenth century, Count of Saint-Martin, entitled one of his books: *The Man of Desire.* I have not read that book, I only know its existence, but I have long felt in its title something magnetic which has helped me in the composition of this volume.

Why should I have added it to the long list of those treating of similar subjects? Ask the many people who have urged me to undertake it. Each generation apparently is anxious to restate its morals, to reconsider its view of life, to test its idea of happiness. Montaigne, full of the Ancients as he was, is however entirely different from them. On the other hand, Anatole France who imitates him recalls his spirit only superficially. Finally Anatole France's successors visualize the same questions from a different angle. In the same way Americans may poke fun at their newspaper philosophers, but they read them, instead of reading Emerson, and I do not skip their wisdom either when the familiar headlines catch my eye. Life is inexhaustible and no observation of it has ever been final.

The reader has probably noticed that the divisions of this book hinted above correspond to the three aspects of "Being" in classical metaphysics: *Verum* (the True), *Pulchrum* (the Beautiful), *Bonum* (the Good). These fine old words will in fact reappear as our sub-titles. But the reader need not fear in this book any metaphysical language more abstruse than that. Even in its first part which cannot but appear rather speculative, its aim is to be practical and jargon will not be admitted into it.

PART ONE

VERUM

THE TRUE

INTRODUCTORY

Why should we begin this introduction to the higher life with something which, after all, will be little else than a summary of the great philosophical questions? Intellectual again. Why not begin with the Beautiful which appeals to everybody, or with religion which, no matter how undermined it is by modern life or by what people call modern science, still permeates our life and the life of our nation? Is it so important that, twenty odd centuries after Aristotle, we should cling to a Greek subdivision when another might be better adapted to our mentality?

The superstition of antiquity has not much force with the present writer, no matter what his ideas may be about a classical education. But there is no more direct way of elevating our life than by elevating our ideas. A friend of mine who was educated at Edgbaston told me that the boys at school there would, in the irreverence of their age, feel inclined sometimes to mimic the aged Newman's everlasting call to his secretary: "Anthony! Anthony!" The moment the quavering voice was succeeded by the appearance of the cardinal's noble, thoughtful head, the mocking mood was replaced by awe. Even boys were conscious that this old man's brain was constantly occupied with meditations on subjects raising mankind high above its usual level. We have all experienced the same feeling. If we come near a person engaged in serious reading, or absorbed in real thought, we know our place at once and we apologize for our intrusion.

Besides, do what we will, we cannot get away from ideas. We cannot speak or act without being conscious of a kind of intellectual tribunal within us ready to sanction or redress what we say or do. This system of notions constantly appealed to may be inherited through education, or it may have been taught us by our successes or failures; it may be conscious or unconscious, but it rules our existence. We call it sometimes our principles, sometimes our philosophy.

We are also aware that any man who possesses a talent or an influence possesses what we call a technique as well. The politician has his technique and the business man has his, both based on a knowledge of psychology. Lawyers and magistrates all systematize a body of practical rules. So do artists. Read Reynolds' *Seven Discourses,* you will realize how carefully thought out, on what solid intellectual basis rests what we may be inclined to regard as a collection of mere recipes.

But this is not all. Behind the technique is something much more general, that is to say applicable to more than one realm: that is the politician's, the business man's, the artist's philosophy. The politician has gathered his from history or from lectures on constitutional law; the business man has risen from economics or publicity to superior notions; all artists are ready to expatiate on the strange relation between lines or colors and the human emotions. Facts have been summed up in conclusions and the conclusions have led to a philosophy, or, as often as not, to philosophy.

When we happen not to feel in somebody we respect the presence of that intellectual substratum we are uncomfortable and on our guard. Why did people follow President Wilson more willingly than Mr. Bryan who was more eloquent? Religionists, eloquent or not, command more influence than mere preachers. Ruskin has awakened more artistic vocations than Reynolds. A philosophy in all these cases has been at work. People are certain that it is not enough to execrate Soviet Russia, that something is alive in Moscow which indignation alone will not crush out. Under the Bolsheviki's tyranny, under their dumping, under their organization, we feel that the philosophy of Lenin, Engels and Marx is a force of a peculiar order. In a familiar phrase, ideas rule the world, and where ideas are lacking no following is seen.

We all, more or less consciously, note this. We cannot help observing that all serious conversations gravitate towards philosophy. Whatever we may declare is our own opinion about life and death, morals or religion, marriage and love, if anybody present unexpectedly shows more knowledge of the literature of the question than we possess, or if he goes back to general principles, we are surprised and perhaps—O supreme mortification!—silenced. Intellect has entered where mere emotionalism, a moment before, was disporting itself, and it takes all the folly of the foolish, after that, to plunge in again with a silly "let me tell you what I think about this". As a rule, the man or woman who happens to have a philosophical basis and has given real thought to the matter under discussion becomes a sort of teacher.

So, our choice is between saying insignificant things, saying nothing, or reading and thinking before saying anything. All important, all fundamental ideas some day must be tested if we want to enjoy the pleasure of feeling secure on the higher intellectual level. We only remember this vaguely when we are adults, but intelligent children have no doubt that it should be so. Many, before reaching their fifteenth year, are intrigued by the overtones accompanying the word philosophy. Not a few, unadvised and unguided, start to build for themselves a philosophy by collecting the deeper sentences they find in Shakespeare or La Fontaine.

This interest lasts during the vital years. Few sophomores read Descartes' life without a wistful longing to shut themselves up at a German inn, as he did, in order to set their intellectual house in order. Even when they do not take a course in philosophy they go some fine morning to the college book-shop and buy one of the many *Introductions to Philosophy* for sale there. Even older people retain a hope that some book some day may lead them to a few intellectual peaks from which they may survey with a calmer eye the field of doubtful questions and know at last what people mean by saying that knowledge is the abolition of fear.

Sometimes the book is found to be helpful and its success takes away the breath of publishers. In most cases the so-called introduction is written in jargon and is full of technicalities. I have read one recently in which a veteran philosopher ranged through the whole vast field of metaphysics, as if anything could be said about insoluble questions and philosophy was only a chance for an old clown of a philosopher, made the nimbler by his own desiccation, to juggle with paradoxes. The result is that perfectly willing and sincere readers, after a trial or two, give up with the verdict: unintelligible, insoluble, idle. In that way, what ought to be a garden of elevating meditations is declared inaccessible for ever.

Is it true that the questions without a comprehension of which we are bound to feel impoverished and inferior are idle, insoluble and unintelligible?

Idle many questions cherished by philosophers undoubtedly are, but they are not the questions at the basis of philosophy. Vital philosophical questions are so far from being idle that not only do all inquiring minds retain their interest in them to the last, but even children wonder about them: "What am I? How is it that I am I and not somebody else?

How is it that I am here? Why and how am I thinking all this? Am I sane in thinking it? Perhaps other people do not wonder about such things. Do I think things as they are or am I only thinking thoughts? Do I really exist? Does the world I imagine I see really exist, or is it all a dream? Is it as I imagine it is, or different? Has it always been here? If not always, why has God created it? How is it that there is room for God and for it, for God and for me?" These questions are, or have been familiar to us. They are not idle, they are vital. Yet, they are the questions asked by philosophy.

Many of those questions are insoluble, or seem to be to-day, but what of that? For many centuries the motions of planets could not be accounted for without clumsy hypotheses; now they are intelligible to school-boys with a modicum of mathematics. Innumerable questions which seemed unanswerable have gradually been answered. Man is recent in our world, remember. Supposing the world to have been seventy years in existence what would be the proportional duration of man's existence? Three days. I am always surprised that mankind should not be more astonished at its own strangeness and uniqueness than it is, and as I shall revert to this on several occasions, I beg permission to insist on it now.

If we could see the Earth as it was a million years ago, one thing would seem prodigious: the absence of man. Many familiar regions would be very nearly as they appear to us, but man would not be there. Life in infinite variety would be visible, but not man. Some animal *might* be imagined to ask the questions enumerated above, but in fact none would, none could. The questions not only would not be insoluble, they would be unasked and the mental world familiar to us would be a blank.

Now think of what is going on in one of our average towns at the present moment. Try to visualize what is being said, discussed, taught, written, printed, read. Think of the laboratories, lecture-rooms and libraries. Think of the enormous sum of knowledge and meditation reposing in one library. Watch the marvels of science. Think of what is going on in churches . . . the wonder of prayer . . .

Little man has done that in his recent bounds forward. Of the billion species on our globe, only his has risen to language and reason, leaving the rest so far behind that the kinship between them is forgotten by all but a few superior minds. Now, questions are asked, eagerly, endlessly asked. Now, solution after solution is propounded, discussed, sometimes declared satisfactory. Little man has acquired an extraordinary knowledge not only of the place where he lives, but of places at incredible distances from him—a truly miraculous development which only our careless familiarity with it can take for granted. How do we dare to speak of insoluble questions?

It is no more true that the great philosophical questions are unintelligible than that they are idle. If they were really unintelligible they would be idle, and we feel that they are vital. Not one of those I mentioned in the list given above is anything but transparent in wording. When people complain of the so-called unintelligibility of philosophy, they complain either of technicalities which are not philosophical, or of the ever-varying vocabulary of philosophers. But probably they ought to complain of their own supineness in not trying to visualize, under their proper angle, questions which are not intelligible when seen in any other light. When people accuse Kant of indulging in jargon for saying that the simple statement: "Alexander was the son of Philip" is a "synthetical judgment" I sympathize to a certain extent. But when the same people declare that Aristotle's famous definition: "Thought is the thought of thought" is unintelligible I do not sympathize. Aristotle's sentence may not be immediately comprehended but it is as intelligible as six times nine is fifty-four, which requires a little more time than two and two make four. People who want immediate intelligibility in all they hear or read cannot hope to go far beyond city-editor copy. All philosophy worthy of the name will be found first of all to be an answer to the fundamental questions which man asks about himself or about the world, and, in the second place, will be found not to require more intellectual effort than poetry. We do not read Shakespeare or Browning as we read the reports of sporting events. We have to forget our trivial environment, for a while, if we wish to reenter the stratum of our consciousness which was habitual to us in childhood. That stratum is both poetic and philosophical: intelligent curiosity or receptivity lives there. Reading poets or philosophers without that kind of collaboration is worse than useless. But with this initial preparation not only lucid philosophers like Locke or Hume, who write in plain forcible English, but even Kant, who does his best with old-fashioned German, will well repay the attention they require. Only they must not be read to *have been* read or even to be remembered, they must be interrogated and listened to.

"How should I go to work?" you ask. *"Do give us practical advice."*

Quite right! First of all an introduction to the higher thought, or to thinking about the higher issues, should be read when you are in the mood for it. You will find it in this book, as humanized and clarified as I have been able to make it. In the second place you should procure, if you do not possess it already, a History of Philosophy and a History of Science which will show you the progress of thought during the last short thirty centuries of the life of mankind. Such a history will lead you naturally to volumes of extracts from the writings of the great philosophers or scientists which are waiting for you in any book-shop. By the time you finish those few books, you will no doubt have begun collecting notes on Personality, Consciousness, Matter, Life, Spirit, the Soul, the acquisition of knowledge, Morals, Free-will, God and the possibility of communicating with God, Religions and the modern criticisms of them.

Those *dossiers,* in a short time, will mean to you not what you know about the vital questions, but what *else* you want to know about them. Whenever you find yourself reaching for them you will also find that you are upstairs, that, possibly unknown to yourself, you have been upstairs for some time. *Verum,* the True, can only be sought high above our daily shabby cares. And do you not notice that there is music in those beautiful ancient words? There is even something more, there is the charm which the early Christians of Greek origin must have found in the talismanic words, the Light, the Way, the Life, which even now mean so much to us in their very vagueness in the Johannine writings. Let us merely repeat them—*Verum, Pulchrum, Bonum*—and we shall shake ourselves free of the littlenesses besetting us. Genius may not whisper its secrets to our inward ear, but we shall be conscious of the blessedness of silence.

SUBDIVISIONS OF PART I

Many text-books of philosophy are divided into three parts under the following titles: Anthropology, Cosmology, Ontology or Metaphysics. Greek words as usual and, as usual, intimidating words to those who do not know Greek, or even to those who do, or once did, or thought they did. But the division is logical, and simple things underlie the long words. Anthropology means an inquiry into Man's nature, Cosmology an inquiry into the Universe, and Ontology or Metaphysics an inquiry into what is beyond both Man and the Universe. It is only because the Greeks were such precursors in everything that their imprint has to be found everywhere.

A. MAN'S INQUIRY INTO HIMSELF

1. *Personality and Its Limits*

That philosophy, or reflection, should begin with Man is natural, for we are conscious of ourselves before being conscious of anything else.

Imagine that, like Milton's Adam, you are suddenly called into existence and find yourself surrounded by the Heavens and Earth with their myriads of entities. You do not know your own name, and the objects around you, never having been named either, retain their virgin newness. Every one of them strikes you as a man of to-day might be impressed by a supernatural apparition. You know no traditions, there are no accretions on anything, nothing that may impair the lucidity of your glance. Everything is just itself, but itself to the full.

In spite of this universal vividness and of a tendency you have to regard all beings as endowed with as much individuality as you possess, something is more vivid to you than it all, and that is yourself. No sensation seems more immediate to you than that consciousness of yourself. Two elements enter into it,—the most vital that you will ever know—first, an urge, as continuous as the flow of your blood, to keep yourself in existence, and, second, the feeling that you are apart from the variegated and fascinating not-you, that you are a person. Both elements, in time, will become so natural to you that they will have to be rediscovered by professional philosophers, yet every time you will be fully cognizant of them they will seem mysterious to you.

"Something mysterious in being a person! Why, I never thought there was anything mysterious about that. Yet, I have been a person for some time."

"Are you sure that you never felt the mysteriousness of being a person? Didn't you, as a child, ask questions which showed that you really did feel it?"

"Oh! you mean the silly questions which children do ask: Why am I Johnny and not Tommy? . . . Why am I not a tree? . . . Couldn't I have been one? . . . How can I be anybody with God being everywhere? . . . All children say those absurd silly things."

"They are not silly, Heaven knows. When children sound silly, you will always find that it is in imitation of their elders. But even grown-ups will sometimes be conscious of the strangeness of being a person. It may only be a few times in their lives, and it may only be in flashes, but practically everybody has had that experience, and most people are awed by it. Have you never been conscious of the space occupied by your body and how inconsiderable it is?"

"Oh! of displacing that little space with me, as I walk, and of being shut up in it? . . . Why, many times."

"That is the sensation I mean. You are then within an ace of realizing that you are an exceedingly fragile bundle of phenomena supported, in some unaccountable way, by a centre, a core which you cannot locate, your Ego."

"Why, I realize that very well, and it is *frightening. All the strength we might derive from the consciousness that we are ourselves is paralyzed by the realization that what makes us a person is, as you say, so slender and impalpable. The more we think of it, the more it seems to shrink into itself, till we are afraid to see it thinning into nothing. I know that feeling of evanescence very well."*

"No doubt, for you describe it pretty well too."

"But why is it frightening like that?"

"Probably because it is the foretaste of our death. What is death? The completeness of the phenomenon you describe. The support of our personality vanishes, and suddenly it is independent of its familiar phenomena. The simile of the soap-bubble is well-chosen. The more we think of our personality, the more afraid we are to see the bubble dissolve into the brilliant morning."

"Yes, evidently, we dread to move from the outside world which supports us so far inwards that we shall be conscious of nothing except our ephemeral selves. I once met at a sleepy boarding-house near the British Museum, in London, a weird old sea-captain whom what we are saying causes me to remember. He had never known, he assured me, anybody brave enough to go to a lonely place at night by himself, to call his own name out loud three times. Realizing one's own personality in that way, no matter how simple, he thought was beyond human endurance."

"Personality is the consciousness at the same time of our self and of the universe outside us which presses against it. We cannot think of personality without having it brought home to us that inevitably the pressure will, some day, force it out of the picture."

"What do I get by thinking of all these depressing things?"

"A little more light about the fact of your existence which is the foundation of all knowledge. If you thought more about it, as a fact, you would not be depressed much longer. Medical students are only afraid of diseases at first."

2. *Story of Personality*

That we are in the world, but not part of the world, is what the psychological analysis in the foregoing chapter has told us. Science can tell us a little more. During the past few decades biology and palæontology have made prodigious strides, and mere psychology is now helped by an historic background which may not be an explanation of the mystery of personality, but without which there would be no hope of an explanation.

Biology is the study of life. There are on our globe millions of living beings, plants or animals, which nourish themselves, grow, reproduce themselves. They are healthy or sick, normal or abnormal. Biology studies these functions and conditions. Occasionally living organisms show variations, spontaneous or artificial, and biology strives to determine the laws of those variations. Such researches offer no particular difficulty and are carried on by many thousands of students at the present moment.

But biologists endowed with more than the average curiosity, and not satisfied with just cataloguing phenomena, are interested in something more fundamental than phenomena. What they want to know is not merely how life acts, but what life is. What makes living organisms so different from inorganic bodies? Here are two gelatinous bits of substance, consisting of the same components,—hydrogen, azote, carbon,—and strikingly alike in appearance. One is alive, the other is not: what makes the living one so different from the other? Aided by the microscope and availing himself of all the resources of chemistry, the biologist, with infinite patience, follows life to its apparently primitive unit, the cell. What makes the cell alive? What makes cells develop according to their own law so that one will become an oak, another a water-flea, another an elephant? How can it be that in the infinitesimal blob are summed up the hereditary characteristics of two families and the future development of a human being? A man is in that droplet, with the cast of his features, the pigments of his hair and skin, the larynx arrangement which will give him the bass voice of his father, or the even more mysterious relation which will make him irritable like his great-grandfather. A whole human existence is summed up in this embryo. Genius or crime may be latent in it. What causes that? What is that mysterious quality which we can name but cannot define, life?

Like biology, palæontology follows life from its more complicated to its simpler elements. It tells a wonderful story, and one cannot help being sorry for such a man as Aristotle for having had no suspicion of geology. On the geological strata, as on a pack of index-cards which some accident might have crumpled edges upwards, the story of life on our planet is written. Yesterday man was not here, only his unknown ancestor; the day before, there were no quadrupeds, only reptiles and birds; the day before that, only fishes or shell-fishes; finally traces are found of even simpler organisms till we come to the beginning of the series, the formless *amœba.*

Can the story be told chronologically instead of backwards? Can we say that *amœbae* developed into shell-fishes and fishes, that the fishes were transformed into birds and reptiles, out of which developed quadrupeds, finally that some quadruped was the ancestor of both the ape and pre-man? If the evolutive theory, in spite of the strong scientific objections made to it, is the most satisfactory, the elemental formless creatures in which life was first manifested contained the germ of what we now witness. In other words the story cell-to-man which biology tells us is repeated by palæontology.

What were the chapters of that wonderful but mysterious story? Nobody knows: but it would be unwise to say that nobody will ever know. No doubt sensibility was the beginning of the relation between the living organism and the world around. Later on vision came. It is surprising that so many people should never wonder about that marvellous phenomenon. That our nerve centres should register cold or heat, pleasurable or painful sensations, is wonderful enough; but that the sense of touch should have become perfected to the point it has reached in the eye, that the world should be mirrored in it and photographed in our memory, as it is, is the marvel of marvels. Without this development, man would have been impossible and science would be inconceivable.

The next stage must have been wonderment. Some day, in the primeval past, our humble ancestor after eating sweet berries bit into a crab-apple, made a face, threw the apple away, but instead of looking merely disgusted he seemed surprised. Wonderment, father of thought, was born, and, ever since, man has never ceased to wonder and think. What the results are the story of civilization, science, art and religion tells in a thousand chapters. Those chapters are entrancing, but not one of them can rival for intellectual possibilities or endless reserves of admiration the bare head-line which sums up them all: from the cell to Newton.

"But what is the connection between this—no matter how marvellous—story, and personality?"

"Personality is the knowledge that we are apart from the rest of the universe. Our body is made out of the same elements that are in the earth or in the stars, it is part of the world. But our life is something apart, and our consciousness is even more separate. Alone of all animals we can double ourselves up, so to speak, to look at ourselves."

"Don't you think that animals are conscious of their personality too?"

"In a way. But they do not know the great secret that we do know and hate knowing—that we shall die—and without that knowledge the consciousness of personality cannot be complete."

3. *Limitations of Human Knowledge*

"You say that knowledge is essential to personality. But is not human knowledge practically boundless with an ever-extending field before it? If so our personality would also extend indefinitely."

"The word knowledge has various meanings which you probably know. When it connotes our intellectual acquisitiveness its meaning becomes singularly restricted."

"Are you going to discourage me? dazzle me perhaps. Philosophers are dangerous. They make one feel like a fool."

"We don't want to look like fools, but we don't want to be ignoramuses either. Of late, philosophers have been mostly scientists or mathematicians. They are young, clean-shaven, gay, bubbling and unconventional. They are close to their facts and antagonistic to traditional nonsense. They are not always sure about the conclusions of their sciences, but they seem sure about their principles. So, we are inclined to imagine that philosophers' philosophy is superannuated. But it is not, and we cannot ignore the obsessing debates of past generations over the capacity of our poor brains to get in touch with something beyond themselves. Surely you know the names of Hume, Berkeley, Kant . . . !"

"Yes, terrifying."

"Never be terrified. There is no reason to be terrified. The aforesaid gentlemen lived perfectly happy lives in spite of their ideas. So can we. We cannot afford to skip a momentous phase in philosophy and there is a good deal of truth in what those great qualifiers have to say."

"There must be: otherwise those philosophers would not occupy all that space in large text-books. Well then, go ahead. I know you're going to begin with: we cannot even be sure of our own existence because . . ."

"No! no philosopher ever dared to say that, no matter how he may have pined to say it. Your radical sceptic does not go further than that you cannot be sure that your Ego is something substantial because you can never study it at rest. Watch your consciousness as much as you like, it will always be passing through some new phase like the brook which is never for two seconds identical with itself. For one fraction of a second you will be conscious of something pleasing, in the next you will be conscious of something annoying; you will want to play with one thing, then you will want to shake away another; you will imagine, then you will remember, and suddenly you will catch yourself combining and reasoning. What does that mean? That our consciousness is a chain of events, not a substance."

"What! when I am annoyed by one thought and try to think another, is it not my Ego that does it? Am I not the cause of the change?"

"Hume says not. He says you have no right to say you see anything except juxtaposition. He does not believe in any causes. Your mind has taught you something which it calls a cause, but you must not be deceived by a mere word. There is no cause and there are no effects, only a succession of events."

"Was not Hume just a boy when he said that, and did he not pretty early shelve philosophy to take up history and fill volume after volume with causes and effects?"

"He certainly did. But there is no evidence that he ever gave up his original notion. If you read his Essays—which are as clear as daylight and capital reading—you will have no doubt about that."

"This shows that philosophy is one thing and life is another: philosophy of that kind is entirely a thing of the inside of the head."

"Not badly put! only remember that mathematics is that too, a thing of the inside of the head with a vengeance, yet every now and then physics uses it, and before you can say Jack Robinson, the thing is light in your drawing-room or heat in the kitchen."

"Look here! couldn't you, couldn't people who insist on this kind of hair-splitting make just that distinction, deal separately with what is purely speculative—I am trying to be polite—and what has a certain amount of practical truth in it?"

"You know perfectly well that a philosopher will never do that; he is a philosopher because he never thinks of utility, of what you call practical truth. But you can discriminate as much as you like and I shall help you. Do you believe in your sensations?"

"Do I believe that blue is blue? Yes."

"Well, you're wrong, for many people, who do not suspect that medicine calls them Daltonians, see blue where normal people see green. Yet they think themselves the normal people and it takes the spectroscope to prove to them that they are not. They give in because physics is one of the modern queens. As philosophers they might go on proclaiming that their blue is the real blue and other people's green is a delusion. They need only say that Man is the measure of all things. But can man be called the measure of things when his own senses contradict one another?"

"My senses behave themselves. I never noticed any contradiction."

"No! cross two fingers, roll a pea, one pea, between them: your sense of touch will report two peas while your vision will go on perceiving one."

"Yes, but my reason will know all the time that my eye-sight is acting under normal conditions while my touch is grossly taken in. So, if you don't mind we shall leave this anti-sensationalism in the category of speculation or hot air."

"You are in a decisive mood, I can see. But do you believe in your ideas, do you believe that your idea of greenness, for instance, is legitimate, or do you think, with Hume, that greenness is only a weakened memory of green things, green leaves, a green dress, green envy or anything green?"

"My idea of green is vivid when I think of bright green, it is not when I think of pale green; there's nothing more to it."

"How unphilosophic! You would collapse if I were to ask you if your idea of *pale* green is vivid. For, as an idea, it ought to be as vivid as your idea of bright green. The question is: what right have you to separate greenness from the many green things you have seen in the course of your life? If greenness to you is only the jumbled recollection of whatever green has been registered by your eyes, you do not believe in ideas, you only believe in sensation and many people do not even believe in that as resolutely as you do."

"Have you seen the poor lark fascinated by the sportsman's mirror? In two minutes I may be that lark. You might shoot me a dozen times, but you would shoot a person who certainly was not in a condition to philosophize. If I were I should daze and fascinate you too, and our debate would go on till the end of the world. Has not that happened in the world of philosophy before?"

"A sceptic's argument against scepticism, but it has its value. However, will you be more philosophic if I ask if you believe in the number seven or the number twelve?"

"Somehow I am more accustomed to old twelve, because things go by dozens. Why, of course I believe in twelve. There's twelve on the calendar because of the twelve months. Or walk into a shop and you will see twelveness associated with whiteness and roundness and, I hope, freshness, in a box of eggs. Twelve is all over the place."

"But is twelve in the box or in your mind? How close must twelve things be in order to produce what you call, so profoundly, twelveness? If there are six eggs in a box and six in the next where is twelve?"

"In my mind, but also in the two boxes on the counter."

"You think so because we are now speaking of twelve. Two people who were talking of the Yale game as they walked into the shop would never think of twelve, they would think of six twice repeated."

"Which is twelve. If one of those people wanted a

dozen eggs, he would not hesitate, he would say: here it is, here are twelve eggs, here is twelve!"

"Which proves that twelve is in the mind and not in reality. Twelve is an idea. By dint of applying that generalization to things grouped in twelve, months for instance, or eggs, or apostles, you get used to the figure, but the eggs do not know that they are twelve, the months will probably be thirteen in the reformed calendar, and the Apostles thought there were twelve of them even when one or two were away. Ideas, things inside the head with no reality in the things themselves. Hume is right again: juxtaposition does it. If you had only seen one green thing in your life and it were an emerald, you would have a memory, a photograph of an emerald but no idea of greenness."

"You suspect, I hope, that I see the lark-mirror twirling all the time. There is no earthly use in all this talk."

"Don't be so sure. Whatever takes us away from common ways of thinking, from our habit of taking things for granted, of never doubting, never wondering, never varying our angle of vision, takes us away from non-thought. However, I am ready to admit that ninety-nine in a hundred professional philosophers, that is to say, professors of philosophy, would regard this conversation merely as practice in thinking, intellectual disciplining. It is partly that, too, that we encounter in the very serious discussion of the nature of our mind carried on between Kant and his critics. Have you ever heard of what the ancients called the argument of the calf?"

"Yes! The farmer's daughter takes the calf in her lap the morning it is born and thinks it as dear as a

kitten. So she takes it up again the next day, and the next and the next. When it is two years old and has become a prize-cow the girl can't take the ex-calf in her lap as cow, but reasoning leaves no doubt that she can still take him up as ex-calf. For, on what day should she have found it impossible to lift up the darling? I have also read the argument of the bald man who never can be bald, even when he has not a single hair left on his head, because his playful wife only pulls out one hair the first day and he cannot be called bald, one hair the next day and he cannot be called bald, and so on ad infinitum. *I am sure anybody with a little technique could put his finger on the weak point of those fooleries and fix, in an excellent formula, the day the calf can no longer be lifted up or the gentleman is declared bald. There would be no date, but there would be a formula, and this shows all the practical use there is in those so-called arguments. Words, words, words."*

"No, not words. Something like mathematics. Read any philosopher and you will be conscious of the mathematical procedure even if there is no mathematics under discussion. Philosophy, like mathematics, always seems to pull down the blinds and turn on light of a special kind. It may not be artificial, but it is not everyday light either. These arguments which amused the sceptics of antiquity place you in that particular light: that is something. But there is more seriousness, in fact, there is nothing but seriousness in what Kant has to tell us about the limitations of our mind. You know the Kantian antinomies?"

"No, I have heard the name, but I have never cared to puzzle over the thing."

"It is not exactly puzzling, it is discouraging. Nobody can like to hear of *fundamental principles entailing wrong conclusions*, or of *a reasoning founded on human reason resulting in an inevitable if not inexplicable illusion.* But Kant's criticism of pure reason cannot be taken lightly. People who pooh-pooh it either have not considered it, or, more probably, have not understood it. In most cases they have not read it. To revert to the antinomies, here is one: Is the world limited in time and space? We can answer: yes or no. Yes, if we answer according to the requirements of our thought; no, if we answer according to the requirements of things. The conclusion is that our mind and what is outside it do not go the same pace."

"I am ready to admit that. Man is no God, and I am only too conscious of the infirmity of my mind. What else does Kant say?"

"You mean: what does Kant chiefly say? For I only mentioned the antinomies to introduce his point of view. The essence of the Kantian criticism is this: in the first place, space and time are conditions rather than realities: we cannot think of anything existing or happening without existing in space or happening in time. But, we cannot be sure that space and time are more than frames in which we picture things. In the second place we organize all our knowledge according to very simple laws without which our mind would be a chaos of notions, for instance: *what is is*, or *a thing cannot be and not be at the same time.* Can we be sure that these laws which are valid for all we know would also be valid for things of which we have no idea? How can we be certain that our investigation exhausts all that is real? That view is the essence of Kantianism."

"Doesn't it mean that I am to be on my guard against every possible statement? Am I to disbelieve science, even though the whole modern world seems to believe in nothing else? How can I mistrust astronomy, for instance, when I see astronomers predicting eclipses, fifty years in advance, and the eclipse happening in just the spot and at just the time settled, with infinitesimal errors?"

"Remember that the astronomers of Ptolemy's school who were all wrong about the solar system also prophesied eclipses accurately. But you are not to disbelieve human science or think human reason invalid except when they venture outside their province. Let me conclude this conversation with two telling statements which will sum up all we should remember of it in order to be what you call 'practical'. Hume calls the Universe of which we have cognizance 'a singular effect', that is to say something which might be entirely different elsewhere. And Pascal who was not heterodox admits that our knowledge of the world is limited to *quelque apparence du milieu des choses*, a superficial knowledge of the centre of things."

"I am entirely willing to admit that, or submit to that. But tell me: are there no philosophers who keep away from the discouraging side of this philosophy?"

"There are Intellectualists like St. Thomas Aquinas—who is almost as much in fashion now as he was seven hundred years ago—who believe in reason and reasoning, in spite of such antinomies as free will and the prescience of God. And there are

Voluntarists like Duns Scotus, or, in the nineteenth century, Maine de Biran, who build their philosophy on the will rather than on the intellect, and so partly protect themselves against the criticism of reason. But it is only partly. The moment the intellect is probed separately, restrictions are bound to appear. I am glad you realize that they are of a different order from the scepticism to which I introduced you at first. That is only a preparation, a sort of Masonic initiation in a chamber of mirages in which nobody should linger. If you admit that there is a philosophic angle of vision under which nothing can appear to you as it did when you did not wonder or doubt, it is enough."

"So philosophy is doubt."

"Or wonder, interrogation. Not taking things for granted."

B. MAN STUDIES THE UNIVERSE

The previous chapters have shown us man's inquiry into himself. He has been described as conscious of his personality or comparative independence of the Universe. Then the capacity of his mind for going beyond mere sensation has been tested. This examination, it must be admitted, has been carried on in an atmosphere of unreality, but it may be unreality to our untrained mind alone.

Now, man turns away from himself to investigate the Universe about him. Material objects, physical laws. We feel more comfortable at once. For though M. Henri Poincaré may tell us that it is as scientific to say that the sun revolves round the earth as that the earth revolves round the sun, we suspect some dodge of the intellect and we go on believing that where facts uniformly confirm laws we are safe in believing in the laws. That is why so many men of an inquiring turn prefer the natural sciences to philosophy, or only begin to philosophize when they have a scientific foundation.

However, it is a fact that metaphysics is constantly lurking beside the path of physics. The moment science has to declare that it cannot give us the last word about even matter, if our curiosity insists on asking more questions the answers have to be given by philosophy. The scientist may refuse to call it by that name, but it is philosophy all the same.

I. *Extent and Duration of the Universe*

THERE unrolls around us the vast universe. We are no longer in the situation of the Egyptian or Chaldean astronomers who, powerful thinkers though they were, had to regard the stars as the "little stars", and thought themselves driven by science to insanity when their calculations brought them to the conclusion that the sun must be as large as a province. Books, articles and lectures, poets' metaphors and orators' comparisons have accustomed us to the immensity of space.

Our planet travels round the sun in a year. The elliptical path it follows at an incredible speed, calculated in miles, dazzles our mind. We see clearly that a thousand human lives could not cope with those distances, and, with the smile of impotence, our imagination gives up the effort. Yet, what our Earth does in a year it takes Neptune, at the frontiers of our system, a hundred and sixty-eight years to complete. Generations vanish and are forgotten, revolutions undo what other revolutions had done, nations rise or decay, science, literature, art pass through decisive phases before Neptune has finished its year. How inconceivably remote from us this almost invisible planet must be! Yet if a chart of the heavens is drawn on such a scale that Neptune will only be four inches from the sun, our own Earth being so close to it and so small in comparison with it that it will be almost invisible, where will the next system appear on the gigantic chart? One mile and a half away. Our solitude is almost unbelievable, and the sentence of Pascal,—awe-inspiring in its nudeness,—comes to mind: *"Le silence éternel des espaces infinis m'effraie."* The eternal silence of infinite space is terrifying.

But beyond the next star, at distances even greater, other stars shine on similarly isolated worlds. No matter how deeply the telescope searches into space, beyond more solitudes more universes can be seen. The light of the sun takes eight minutes to reach us; the light of other stars, comparatively so near that they are familiar, takes hundreds of years, and the beam from them which has just reached us may be contemporaneous with Shakespeare. Indeed, our instruments record to-day astronomical catastrophes which took place about the time when Christ was born. Yet these inconceivable durations corresponding to unthinkable distances are nothing compared with the figures which the final effort of the telescope, assisted by the camera, registers. Some stars are a hundred and forty million light-years away from us. Wait a few more years: the 200-inch telescope being made for the Mount Wilson Observatory will turn its great eye upon those immensities and in a moment more marvels will be revealed.

All this is familiar, but no matter how often we have thought of it, or spoken of it, it is not familiar enough not to send a shiver through our whole mind, wrenching it from its stale conceptions and opening it to views which, to the traditional outlook, would have seemed fanciful but are, in reality, sober philosophy.

How far will the new telescope see? And how far the as yet unsuspected instruments of the future? What will they see? Will our descendants count in billion light-years where we now count in million? Or will there be a halt? Will the ultimate limits of the material universe appear? Einstein demonstrates that space is limited and that its limits are in a curve. Most mathematicians concur in his view. But what is space to our mind? Is it not possible location for more and more matter, whatever its rarefaction may be? If so, why should space be limited, if our mind can add more possibilities *ad infinitum?*

Equally curious is our mind concerning the duration of the material world. Has it always been there? eternally been there? been there without any beginning? that means. The moment it hears this our intellect jibes, for our imagination starts to work and after a few jerky efforts towards that "no beginning" it refuses to try any longer. But logic enters and asks its questions. If the universe never had any beginning, is not its existence an intellectual necessity? But why should mere matter be necessary when our mind, without any effort, can visualize its annihilation? If the universe never had any beginning, constantly building and re-building itself, as it is, is it not necessary to conclude that it must have done so an infinity of times? Ponder the word infinity. It means that no figure can limit it, even should it extend to the furthest away stars which future telescopes will see. That figure would be as nothing compared to infinity. In the indefinite number of combinations possible to a universe of infinite duration, the Earth must have been what it now is an infinity of times; I must have written this page an infinity of times in the abyss of the past; and you must have read it an infinity of times. That is what the mind reads, has to read, in the word infinity.

No, you say, the universe of matter, Space, Time, must have had a beginning.—Must it? Why? By whom then was it created? and what for? Unless your idea of the Creator is purely that of a Superman, the notion of creation may be less repellent to your imagination than that of infinite duration, but it will be repellent to your intellect. Why should a Spirit who, of His own nature, must be conceived primarily as self-sufficient, want to create anything? And why should He create something so antagonistic to Himself as matter? It is not surprising that St. Thomas Aquinas should admit the possibility of regarding the Creator and His creation as a co-eternal cause and effect. This view may entail as many difficulties as the more anthropomorphic concept, but to the modern mind, at least, it seems more in keeping with apparently irrefutable data.

"You see how difficult it is to keep metaphysics out of these questions. Introduce space or time and in an instant even mathematics has to step aside to make room for philosophy."

"Yes, but the problems are insoluble and philosophy knows they are beyond us."

"They would be even more beyond us if they were not considered. The dignity of man lies in his desire to see beyond our material experience."

2. *Nature of the Universe*

"Does it make much difference, after all, if the Universe is boundless or not, if its duration is what scientists say it is or shorter? Size is nothing."

"Are you not practical any more? Surely you must see that our conception of God has been helped by the astronomical discoveries. On the other hand, the vast successions of ages which geology or astrophysics require for their calculations inevitably act upon our imagination and indirectly on our intelligence. It is not indifferent that we should be enabled to give more elbow-room to the actors in the cosmic drama than there is between 4004 B.C. and the present day. The emendations to transformism which have recently been suggested also compel our imagination to suppose on the globe, at various epochs, conditions favorable to sudden changes of which we have no idea at present. Whatever helps us to visualize things as different from what our intellectual sleepiness shows them to be ought to be gladly welcomed."

"I see that, but if I ask the question: 'What is *the Universe, what is it made of, what is its real nature?' I can't see that it makes the least difference if I see it with my naked eye or through the largest telescope, if it is millions of centuries old or if it dates from yesterday."*

"No difference at all. Aristotle was sure that the

heavenly bodies were made of a special substance, infinitely finer than the four elements, which he called quintessence or fifth essence. But the spectroscope leaves us under no such poetic delusions: the stars are made of the bodies familiar to us here below and might be used to manufacture our kitchen utensils."

"Well then, what is the essence of those bodies? What is matter?"

"Have you ever seen Crookes' tubes?

> *'Seen Nature naked, atomic, swift at work,*
> *With fiery sparks fluorescent on her path?' "*

"Yes, I have seen those tubes. It is an experience one does not forget."

"And have you seen a nebula in the telescope?"

"Certainly, and I also see that you are going to tell me about protons, electrons and waves, scattered matter and so forth. Introduce gyration and the primitive nebula will become a vast sphere out of which the stars will be blown,—as the moon was blown out of the sun—like small soap-bubbles out of a larger one."

"No, I will not introduce gyration. It is too much of a problem to understand how it ever introduced itself. And I will not get enthusiastic over electrons, even if I am told that, like angels, they can move from one spot to another and never be found at any intermediary point. Clearly those mathematical revelations are at the same time too abstract and yet too easily mistaken for perfectly simple and intelligible statements, to be for me. But there is one thing in them which seems to force itself upon the mind and stay there."

"The hopelessness of getting at any clear notion of the matter?"

"No, I would rather be positive than negative. I mean the speed with which matter now travels from its former definition. Do you remember what is the Greek for matter?"

"Oh! as Molière's character exclaims,—'For the sake of Greek do, sir, let me embrace you!' No indeed, I do not remember."

"Well it is *ule,* which also meant wood. The Greeks selected the deadest, most inert thing at hand to represent what they thought matter must be. To-day, we are told that matter properly investigated appears to be nothing but electricity, and electricity travels seven times round the earth in a second. The notion of matter evidently tends to become less and less material."

"Which no less evidently does not tend to result in a definition."

"Who knows? This is a time of reconstruction and the work is barely started. However, if inorganic matter is so far from what it was supposed to be, don't you think that organic matter, life, will be even farther?"

"Yes, of course, but do not scientists say that there, too, electricity is the ultimate manifestation?"

"The ultimate manifestation of living cells, perhaps, but not of what makes them alive, not of Life. Surely that is quite apart from matter, even if it is associated with matter."

"You say 'surely', but what is certain in the philosophy of physics? Has not the theory of hormones changed the whole outlook of biology?"

"It has, but I do not think it reasonable to build

on uncertain possibilities. If science is certain of one thing it is of its own uncertainty."

"A state of mind far superior to the unfounded certainties of Fundamentalists, you will admit."

"Yes, but science at times is pretty cocksure. Remember Haeckel. And as his name comes to mind let me ask you what I think is the all-important question. Do you believe, as Haeckel and his many followers did, that with hydrogen, azote and carbon, a living cell can be reproduced in the laboratory?"

"I do not believe it, but I do not disbelieve it either. To be frank I see no impossibility in it."

"Remember that the laboratory has long produced fats which, at first sight, are indistinguishable from organic greases. But they are not organic, any more than a perfect automaton would be a man. Life, mysterious life, is not in them and cannot be forced or coaxed into them any more than the aerial swallow can be wished into the canary's cage. Biologists are not sanguine just now."

"I was only talking logical possibility. You must admit that some day, through some now inconceivable piece of luck, a living cell may be produced at the Rockefeller Institute and kept alive by the Carrels of the day till parts of it can be distributed among the great laboratories all over the world."

"Infinitely doubtful. But suppose this truly living cell *is* created and Promethean biologists from all over the world watch it in its crystal cradle, do you think they could develop it into even an *amœba?*"

"No, for some reason, my mind refuses to admit that possibility."

"Therefore there is even less possibility to see it

develop into an ammonite of any size, and gradually pass through all the transformations which palæontology reads in its chains of living beings."

"No chance whatever."

"Now remember what took place, most undoubtedly took place, on our earth. One day, untold æons ago, the living cell appeared, and now, you and I, its descendants, are having this conversation in which we show ourselves to be the intellectual lords of the world, taking our data from innumerable sources and using them with incredible swiftness. Billions of species, other than our own, have been evolved from the original cell, but have been arrested in their mental development. We know there is no chance for even the most intelligent apes, whereas our own chances for comprehension and mastery seem indefinite. All this marvellous human development was latent in the original cell. Consciousness, sensibility, vision, reason, were latent in it. All that has to be summed up in the world in the great word Mind has been developing at the same time as Life. Finally ideals have become clear and imperious, and the higher levels have been discovered by pioneers of intelligence, art, morals and religion. Is it not evident that, as electricity is superior to dead matter, life superior to atoms, and mind superior to life, there must have been at work in the world something superior to even Mind and that something has been guiding all the development we see?"

"I cannot see how we can conclude differently, unless we fall back on Kant's criticism or on Hume's singular effect."

"Hume's 'singular effect' works in two ways. It can make us distrust our reason, of course, but on the other hand, it can open marvellous possibilities. Astronomers tell us that about a hundred thousand stellar systems seem to be in the same stage as ours, with planets similar to Venus or Mars. Why not remember, with Voltaire, that an ape in another world might be a Newton, while a Newton might conversely be an ape?"

"Painful to think of, but true."

"Painful! I call that possibility marvellous. What would I not give to see a world in which Newtons would be the mob! Imagine what its real Newtons must be! Marvellous, I tell you. Glorious and enchanting! And somehow we cannot help imagining that it must be so. Yet, matter is the same in all the universes we can see, and therefore the spiritual element which works under it must be the same that we see at work on our earth. Only its manifestations are, or must be, superior to all we know or can imagine."

"That is indeed a great vision, and a great idea, and surely *a great certainty."*

"I knew that, in time, you must see it that way. Needless to ask you what is the name of the spiritual element we bow to the moment we glimpse the glory of its manifestations."

"No name is adequate. There is none but is not desperately inadequate. God is the Ineffable."

C. METAPHYSICS

Aristotle's treatises on supra-sensible causes were placed by the Scholiasts immediately after the philosopher's books on Physics. In consequence of this peculiarity they were called metaphysics (*meta*, after).

But the same name can also designate all knowledge superior to physics, so that its modern acceptation is entirely legitimate. Metaphysics is the science which begins to speak when physics has to be silent. We have just seen that the consideration of the Universe in its entirety has led us to a spiritual element which in the universe we call God while in ourselves it is called Mind or the Soul.

Metaphysics deals with that double spiritual aspect of material appearances.

I. God

1. *Existence of God*

If we were told that the beauty of the forest, its poetry, its eeriness, all that we love in it is the work of a beneficent Spirit hidden in its silence or flying on its breezes, we should love the notion. Perhaps we would endeavor to establish a communication with this Spirit. The idea of God acts in the same way on the philosopher's mind. The more he learns about the wonders of creation, the deeper he gets into metaphysics or mathematics, the vaster and the more refined, in a word, his notion of God's works becomes, the more glowing also grows his intellectual happiness. Read Plato or Augustine, read even those cooler logicians, Aristotle or Aquinas. Why is it then that the existence of God is questioned by some thinkers, and is angrily, savagely denied by thousands of men?

The explanation of this strange anomaly is given not by philosophy, but by history. The tradition that Fear created the gods, that primitive man read the existence of the Divinity in plagues rather than in blessings, is still alive and resented. So is the kindred recollection of priestly power. Ecclesiasticism, many people declare, is still with us: not a week passes without some effort on its part to rule even conjugal life in the name of the deity. God has been used, through the ages, by his priests. The more independent people have become economically, the more resolute they have grown to use their independence as they pleased. This inclination, combined with the chances for material satisfactions which our civilization offers at every step, is what is called modern paganism. The expression is faulty, of course, seeing that the pagans were, as Paul called them on the sacred hill of Athens, "all too fearful of the gods", but the wrong word is trying to denote an obvious thing. What this thing is anybody can see: it is the deification of pleasure. Many people who still call themselves Christians are really pagans insofar as they have two gods: one represented by their Church whom they fear and would hate if they dared, the other, Pleasure, whom they adore, or in whom they adore themselves.

But people who resent clericalism or deify pleasure do not, for all that, publicly deny God. This is reserved for people often of a powerfully and rather grossly emotional nature, whose logic is easily affected by their sentiments. Such people have been known, time and time again, to deny God either because they were suffering, or because the suffering of others was unbearable to them. They cannot reconcile the notion of an all-powerful, all-merciful Being with the actual presence of Evil. All they have heard in Christian churches about the goodness of God suddenly seems to them to be a cruel mockery or a brazen lie, and they blaspheme.

"Yes, I remember Swinburne's verses in Atalanta:

'None hath beheld Him, none!
Seen above other gods and shapes of things,
Swift without feet and flying without wings,
Intolerable, not clad with death or life,
Insatiable, not known of night or day,
The lord of love and loathing and of strife
Who gives a star and takes a sun away. . . .

. . . .

The supreme Evil, God!' "

"A strange admixture of force and feebleness. Why did you skip the four or five last verses?"

"Because I do not remember them. And I do not remember them because, as you say, they are feeble and declamatory. Shelley, in Prometheus, *would be better, but I have not read* Prometheus *for years."*

"Yes, there is something in the beginning about requiting knee-prayers with hecatombs of hearts or hecatombs of hopes which sounds more like the real thing. The idea is always the same. God is a tyrant abusing his strength to crush creatures purposely made weak so that they can easily be crushed. God is Evil. But those poetic effusions are not so strong as they are violent: it is only because they are exceptional in literature—not in life—that people quote them with bated breath."

"Don't you think that the problem of Evil is a real problem?"

"The most difficult of problems! but I do not think it expresses itself in literature. It is mostly felt with its full force by people who shake their heads and never say a word."

"That's the way I felt yesterday seeing two boatmen near the Pont-au-Double trying to revive a

drowned man they had just pulled ashore. This was an old man with a pinched face and, even in death, a pitiful expression. Imagine the misery that must accumulate before a man makes up his mind not to see the noon of a beautiful day in May. But this is one incident in a thousand. Shelley is right. Hecatombs of hopes. When the idea comes to mind the brain becomes as numbed as the heart."

"Only too true. If we could see the amount of wretchedness, moral as well as physical, which each minute produces, the suffering of man and animal, the disappointments, the treasons, the deceit and the corruption, the multiform cruelty to young and old, even to small children, the failure of noble attempts, the relapse into hated habits, the constant defeat, in a word, by Evil of what we call God, not only our faith in theism would be shattered but our minds would not stand the shock. If evil were not hidden like impure germs disseminated in our system, there would not be a single sane person on earth."

"You just said that God is constantly defeated by Evil. Does not this amount to an admission that there is no God?"

"No! merely an admission that there are mysteries. This one is the most oppressive because its background is misery, human misery. You must have read many times that science is supremely pessimistic as the end it foresees for the universe is destruction perhaps followed by more efforts resulting in more catastrophes, but probably this prospect does not affect you as ten minutes in a cancer hospital would be sure to do."

"It does not because somehow I imagine that by that time things will be righted. Infinite prospects

are only blanks and there is no terror in them. But how do you reconcile yourself to the mystery of evil?"

"By thinking of the mystery of Good! One should never be polemical about anything serious, above all about anything religious. But suppose you are attacked, by one of the few scoffers left, on this very question of the existence of God being disproved by the prevalence of evil, you can silence him at once—not of course persuade him—by asking him to account for the existence of Good if there is no God."

"You mean that the same arguments which have led us to the conclusion that there must be a spiritual other side to the world can be used again about this issue?"

"I mean that if matter can result in spirit, if its selfishness can naturally be transmuted into disinterestedness, if the play of atoms can in time produce the life of Christ, *plus* can be said to come out of *minus*, and our reason is a mirage. The whole thing can be said in two words, but it can also provide material for a life-long meditation."

"I see, in fact, that Materialists have used up whole existences in trying to imagine plus *coming out of* minus. *And I know that, more and more, Science gets away from the simplicity of mechanicism. But are there no arguments against the existence of God except the existence of evil?"*

"There are. Nobody has set them forth with more vigor than Kant, and you can read his criticism of the classical proofs in the *Critique of Pure Reason.* It is not easy to answer it."

"Well then?"

"Well, Kant himself was not affected by them!

Nobody can have believed in God more wholeheartedly than he did."

"How?"

"He knew that his criticisms were only philosopher's philosophy. His own belief, like Newman's, had a deeper root than mere reasoning. To him belief in God and belief in the moral law were one thing. This means that he, too, could not solve the mystery of Good without bowing to a divine fountain of goodness."

"Yes, does not Kant say also that we will *the existence of God more than we infer it?"*

"He does. But which of our human beliefs,—I mean truly human beliefs, not logical convictions,—is not a choice? Scrutinize your own soul, scan your principles, you will find that love, preference, inclination are at work under your apparently purely intellectual conclusions. All theologians admit that logic is only a preparation to faith. The final assent comes from the impulse of the will. If theologians could express their generally excellent psychology in the language of literature they would be more convincing than they are. Newman's *Grammar of Assent* has a terrible title, but it is convincing psychology expressed in the most beautiful language. Read the book."

"I will."

2. *Nature of the Divine Being*

"If I understood rightly what you said about the existence of God, the Divine Being ought to be defined as an explanation of the universe."

"*The* explanation of the Universe would be better, but it would still imply that God might be a mere intellectual necessity, a concept like Space or Time. God is the spiritual element without which the Universe could neither exist nor be understood."

"Is that what most people think God is?"

"Of course not. Most people means, I suppose, the majority of people. Now you know that the majority of people have a very inadequate idea of God."

"Who has an adequate idea of God?"

"Nobody. Even a genius on one of those globes where a Newton would seem an ape would have no adequate idea of God. The measure of perfection cannot be seized in its entirety by anything that is not perfect."

"Does this mean that no sacred book, not even the Bible, can give us an adequate idea of God?"

"How could they? Is not the human language full of limitations? Even Sunday School children now-a-days make their own inward reservations when they hear that God walked in the garden in the cool of the day, ordered massacres, or had bears devour children who had made fun of an old prophet. The most uneducated readers of the Bible realize that the notion of the Divine Being is purer in *Isaiah* than in *Judges,* and purer again in the New Testament."

"Yes. I know that all this is felt even when it is not actually expressed. But should we infer that the notion of God is in perpetual progress?"

"In spite of its ethical or devotional implications the notion of God is intellectual and, as such, is better grasped as the human mind becomes more capable of grasping it. Many people object to that view because they either imagine that it detracts from the sovereignty of God or insist that God, being the God of all, must be equally understood by all."

"There is something pretty appealing in this."

"No doubt. Belittling anybody's God is cruel and criminal. But the sacred name is charged with a heavy heredity. Remember that it is still written by millions of people with a small letter, and the Hebrews often saw only a difference of power, not of nature, between their Iahve and the Baal of their neighbors. So it is not surprising that the word God should share in the destinies of all words and be partly understood by a few men, misunderstood by most."

"I once read that Diderot would say to the people of his day: 'Enlarge your God!' No doubt he meant: broaden and elevate your notion of God."

"Yes, but living just before Goethe, the most modern of moderns, he was deeply impressed by the astronomical discoveries and his idea probably was: let there be no geocentrism or judeocentrism in your notion of God when our Universe has just been made so vast that we cannot conceive its limits. It is a fact that the larger the effect the larger the cause must seem to us. The final word should be: let there be as little anthropomorphism as possible in our notion of God, eliminate from it what is of man, that is to say material, and bring it as near as possible to the notion of pure Spirit."

"What is a Spirit?"

"I was awaiting this question rather anxiously. Luckily you asked it in the proper subdued tone and not in the confident way of people who either imagine that there can be no answer or that the answer must be the simplest thing in the world. You realize that, on our globe where Newtons are the supreme effort of nature and yet write queer commentaries on *Revelation,* a definition by the partly material of the purely spiritual is an impossibility. All we can do is to say what a spirit is not. And the best we can do is to go on wondering what a spirit really is."

"Can we say much more than that a spirit is not material?"

"That means that a spirit is not bounded as we are by the two great tyrannical categories: Space and Time. All we see is limited by space and all we do, nay, all we are, is limited by time. If there were not so much joy in getting at the truth, even the unpleasant truth, the thought of our imprisonment in space and time would be unbearable. A pure Spirit, God, all the time sees the whole picture of which we only see fragments. The Universe, even the endless succession of universes which astronomy has sometimes inferred from the conservation of energy, is present to Him as our consciousness of ourselves, at a given moment, is present to us. Have you noticed that even everyday parlance prefers to say that God *sees* everything rather than that He *knows* everything? To know implies the action of the memory which refers to the past and is a poor makeshift for constant and direct vision. It is remarkable that the common language should be so accurate whereas the popular notions of God are gross."

"Is there no possibility of a relatively pure, almost mathematical, notion of God apart from philosophy? If so, is it not a pretty discouraging idea?"

"Keep emotionalism out of such questions, if you want to get anywhere. But you know that mystics have seldom been mathematicians or metaphysicians. In most cases they are simple people endowed with an extraordinary gift. They invariably surprise the professional philosopher by the sublimity of their conception of God. Therefore it is not true to say that, apart from high intellectualism, men are condemned to an inferior notion of the Spirit. Contemplation, the interior life, life on the higher levels, is possible to all of us, and, in all of us, it can produce its marvellous effects."

"Contemplation, as you seem to understand it, is a religious act, is it not? It is an effort, as spiritual writers often put it strangely, to see God face to face. Now isn't that anthropomorphism with a vengeance? What can the face of a spirit be? On the other hand, if you try to get away from anthropomorphism you are promptly compelled to admit that a spirit cannot be a person. A person is a person because of differences, is he not? Now, a spirit occupying no definite point, showing no limitations, no characteristics, cannot be differentiated. Therefore God is not a person as we conceive a person to be."

"Excellently put! God is *not* a person as we conceive a person to be. But should the next step be that God is not a person at all, that He is impersonal?"

"Many people are pantheists and so dissolve God through the Universe that it is as if there were no God."

"Precisely. Now, admire once more what words can do, how the least absentmindedness in analyzing their meaning can lead us away from the truth. Do you think it logical to say that since God is not a person, as we conceive an ordinary person to be, He is impersonal? What is the usual meaning of the word impersonal?"

"Indefinite."

"Indefinite to the point of being non-existent, you mean?"

"Perhaps not quite so much as that. Indefinite to the point of not being to be bothered about."

"Exactly. Indefinite to the point of being severely let alone. Some day[1] we shall inquire into the tendency many people show to regard the loss of God as if it were a marvellous gain. Just now what I want to say is that it is illogical to conclude that, since God is not a person as we conceive a person to be, He should be let alone, ignored. There is no question of religion here, mind you, only of logic. Which do you think has more personality: Shakespeare or Pinero?"

"Ask the theatre fireman."

"Yet, is it not true that Pinero occupies a more definite point of literary space than Shakespeare?

---

[1] See Part III, section B, Chap. II.

Are not his characteristics more easily described because they are more restricted?"

"They are. You can give any foreigner an idea of Pinero's work in two minutes, whereas it takes hours and great talent to characterize Shakespeare. The simpler the object is, the simpler its description is likely to be."

"Would you also say: the smaller the man is the more personal he should be?"

"Have I been absurd anywhere?"

"You have been unguarded in your use of the word personal, that's all. The less limited we are, or the less we feel the pressure of environment and heredity, in short, the less we look, speak and act like our father or like the people in our town, the more personal we are. Now, *ex hypothesi,* God does not feel the pressure of the Universe in the remotest manner. Multiply Shakespeare by the infinite and you will have some faint human idea of the personality of God. Have you ever read in any textbook that Aristotle defines God as pure act, *actus purus?"*

"Dozens of times. But it is one of those scholasticisms from which I run away in terror."

"*Actus purus,* a scholasticism! Blasphemy, blasphemy! *Actus purus* is not a formula. To me it is a sort of gem in which I see more fascinatingly human things than have ever been conjured into four syllables by any Oriental enchanter. And do not doubt that Aristotle saw those things too: the divine, the divinely happy, condition of a Being who never can wish for anything because all the time He enjoys everything. Imagine an artist whose inspiration was ceaseless and continuously followed by realization.

A Shakespeare or a Beethoven constantly at his best. All we can do to form an idea of God's personality should be in that direction, removing limitations all the time. That is prayer and that is adoration!"

"I will never blaspheme against actus purus *any more. I had no idea that poetry could be extracted out of a Latin formula."*

"Formulas, apparently abstract formulas, in a dead language, are apt to seem metallic and lifeless. Look at them long enough to see what the inventor thought and saw before he finally condensed the contemplation of a life-time in their syllables and suddenly you will discover that they are sesames to enchanted halls. What do you say now about the personality of God?"

"That our own personality is a remote reflection, an infinitely weak copy of it."

"Yes, but expect millions of people to go on imagining that, if God is personal, He must be a not exactly lovable old person with a beard. Aged words, superannuated associations, even the art and poetry of the past combine to deceive us in such matters."

It is a common saying that a little knowledge takes man away from his belief in God but deeper knowledge brings him back to it. And some wit once remarked that when this happened it was not the same God that was believed in.

Nothing flippant can ever be absolutely true and the present saying is no exception. However keen the pleasure which irreverence may find in the mention of two gods there can only be one God. Human conceptions vary with individuals. Folly, levity or stupidity produce ridiculous notions; thought and the passion for truth seldom fail to get their reward. In no case more strikingly than in the quest after God.

II. The Soul

"Soul" is one of those many words which, in the course of their eventful existence, have not been able to preserve their identity.

To modern ears the soul is rather the vital principle keeping organic matter together than the higher faculties enabling us to reason and organize. Nobody ever speaks of a soulful scientist. The word has even ceased to describe the highest kind of poetry accurately.

So, when we refer to our most intellectual apprehension we now prefer the words *mind* or *consciousness.* However "soul" possesses such a rich heritage of allusion, it has been clad in such a rainbow scarf of poetry since Psyche made her entrance into the world of imaginative reason, that it is difficult and it does not seem desirable to avoid it. Keep it out of the problems of immateriality, immortality or free will, and mankind will feel impoverished and cheated.

1. *Immateriality of the Soul*

The materiality or immateriality of the soul has been discussed for three thousand years. Democritus and Epicurus could not conceive of anything that was not reducible to atoms. So, to them, the soul was an aggregate of infinitesimals. Consequently it was not different from the rest of the material universe.

This reasoning would be cogent if it did not beg the question. Also, to us moderns, if it did not conflict with the recent atomic theories showing us even light as consisting of corpuscles because the corpuscles, instead of appearing as small shot, are now waves of energy.

This applies to the brain even more than to chemical bodies. Nobody is prepared to state that mental operations are performed apart from the brain, but, on the other hand, few people now-a-days dare to say that thought is exclusively produced by modifications in the gray matter. The behaviorist who tells you that thought is only an inward sort of speech may be as affirmative as he pleases, he is not convincing. Materialism—or to give it its elegant new names, mechanism or naturalism—is not in favor with contemporary scientists. Its chief support has been taken away from it.

"How then do philosophers who prefer the opposite doctrine think of the spirituality of the soul?"

"Did I notice a certain ring in your question? You remember, do you not, that, as Pascal says in discussing this very issue, there is no zeal here of spiritual devotion?"

"Often is, though, especially when clergymen happen to be the philosophers. We suspect that, if the soul is declared to be spiritual, the next step will be to threaten us with hell or coax us into heaven."

"It may be the fault of the zealous ecclesiastics, but it may also be the poor logic of their interlocutors. At all events, *we* are trying to approach philosophy philosophically. Your question was: what is the philosophical foundation for a belief in the spirituality of the soul. My answer is this:

1. modern physics sees energy everywhere in the world;
2. biology sees something more spiritual than mere energy in life;
3. philosophy can hardly help seeing something even more spiritual than life in Mind, the supreme achievement of nature."

"But is it not everlastingly true that, if you destroy the brain, you also destroy the mind?"

"What of that? Destroy matter you destroy energy or, at all events, its visibility. If the universe were destroyed there would not be a trace left of the miracle of evolution. The mind works in the brain as energy works in the world. But if you say that the world *is* energy or the brain *is* mind, you beg the question."

"This means that you leave to Materialists the burden of proving that the soul is not *immaterial."*

"If you like, although I hate even the appearance of tactics in such an issue as this. What I mean is that, if I cannot see spirit at work in my mind as I see it at work in the universe, I am left with my note of interrogation and the materialist alone stands before me with his unshaken certainty. All he has to give me is his everlasting: There is only matter in the world indefatigably repeated, although physicists shake their incredulous heads."

"So you would rather be with the physicists who have some arguments on their side than with the materialists who have only their belief?"

"Beautifully put. Final. Yes, materialism seems to me to be a faith."

2. *Immortality*

"But is not immortality also a faith?"

"Pomponazzi, in the sixteenth century, was in hot water for saying so. You can read the story in Bayle's dictionary: three lines of not very interesting text at the top of the page, column after column of exciting notes just below, and the margins full of references. Great work. There you will see how Pomponazzi, finding that Aristotle believed the soul to be corporeal, pointed out to his Aristotelian *bêtes noires* that *their* belief in immortality could only be based on the authority of the Church."

"I am surprised. I thought Aristotle was always on the side of the angels. But is it not true that immortality and religion are interdependent?"

"The ancient Hebrews did not think so. You have to travel through a good deal of Biblical literature before you can be sure that the authors had no doubts about a future life."

"Yet, surely belief in immortality is connected with belief in God?"

"Ah! that is much better put than that religion is dependent on belief in immortality. You can believe in God without believing in immortality, but it is hard to see how anybody can believe in immortality and not believe in God. Have you read Plato's Dialogues on the subject?"

"Oh! just Phædo, *and so long ago. . ."*

"Well, the main idea is that, unless the soul has time, in another life, to be purified of its sins, Evil is victorious over Good, or, as we should say, the Devil is victorious over God."

"Simple, convincing, and terse. I love a reasoning of that kind."

"Then you will also like the parallel doctrine developed by the Neo-Platonists."

"You mean Plotinus?"

"Plotinus and Porphyry both lay great stress on what they call *anagōgē,* the ascent of the soul towards its Maker. No life is long enough, or favorable enough, to make this ascent possible for any of us. The conclusion is obvious."

"Can we not say too that, if there is no future life, human suffering is all in vain,—a hideous thought,—while injustice is not redressed, which sounds immoral? Is this philosophy, or is it mere sentiment?"

"It must be philosophy, for it is exactly Kant's second postulate. Treat it as mere sentiment and the philosopher's system will be in great danger of collapse."

"Now, let me be frankly sentimental. Unless I can think that animal suffering, the long martyrdom of so many poor creatures cannot be in vain either, my idea of God is obscured by the same objections which the vision of any kind of injustice raises."

"The cartesian view of animals as machines, and the modern so-called scientific view that man's life is so precious that other lives may be remorselessly sacrificed to it, appear to me equally laughable. So I am strongly inclined to think that if annihilation seems to us good enough for animals it is largely on account of our exaggerated appreciation of ourselves. However, remember—in order to avoid unnecessary anguish,—that animals live in the present: they never think, as we do, of the suffering in store for them, above all they are spared the torture familiar to man, the clear vision of death."

"Perhaps. Yet the resignation of animals is sad, inexpressibly touching and sad."

"So is that of many men and women who know what real misery is. Wherever we look we encounter an earth where suffering outweighs happiness, and where perfection is only intelligible to us as the negation of endless imperfection. The same divine influence which we see at work in what we can guess of the past cannot stop now. Once more remember the days in the Tertiary Age when there was not a single thought produced on our globe. Then contrast that vacuum with our civilization and knowledge. Why not imagine that even more extraordinary steps onward will be made in the coming ages? Surely nothing can be more philosophical than to supplement our philosophy with the hope of future knowledge. Immortality, which to Cicero was only a beautiful vision, something to enchant oneself with, seems a necessity to Kant, and its demonstration may be perfect long before another two thousand years have elapsed."

D. MORALS OR THE METAPHYSICS OF RIGHT AND WRONG

THE origin and the foundation of morals have always been discussed. "Why do you say: this is wrong?" is an old question. But ethical issues have never been discussed as hotly as they are now. Look at the bookseller's windows. Philosophy proper, prehistory and sociology all handle and rehandle the hows and wherefores of morals in a hundred ways.

"You know the main currents of opinion, of course."

"I know that many people rebuild morals on the old utilitarian foundation but call it sociological. I am told that if I slay not it is because I dread to be slain in my turn; I do not steal lest the custom of thieving should extend to my own property; I do not lie because I hate to be deceived myself. All I do that I call right is, in that way, shown to be what I find necessary or useful. The basis, as well as the summary, of morals are declared to be expressed in the perfectly philistine saying: honesty is the best policy."

"Don't you think that, ignoble as this view of the origin of morals sounds, there is a great deal of truth in it?"

"Why, it is undeniable. All the time we catch ourselves doing right because it is advantageous. But it is not the whole explanation. I admit that I feel the pressure of social necessities at a great many points. But a thing may be at the same time right *and* advisable, wrong and inexpedient. The simultaneity proves nothing. It is certainly not because I am afraid of the effects of drunkenness that I take my wine with moderation. Nor is it merely because I might make a fool of myself. It is because I should be ashamed of myself."

"Is not that egotistical too, in a certain sense? It is in our interest that we should not be ashamed."

"Yes, but it is not in my interest to lose my life by trying to save a drowning child, or by fighting for my country, or by volunteering for a dangerous scientific experiment. Where can my interest in such actions be? They undoubtedly could never be done were it not for a conviction, somehow acquired, that principles are more important than even life."

"Aren't you afraid that these so-called principles may be more or less reducible to some superior form of egotism, the craving for admiration, for instance? The athlete is admired for his prowess, the warrior is admired for his bravery; in that way a tradition sustained by poetry and by the arts is created. In time it seems better, opinion actually declares it is better, to risk or even lose one's life than forfeit admiration."

"Probably that is true. But is not this kind of egotism superior to the egotism which consists in saving one's skin at all costs?"

"It is superior in our view."

"Well, that shows, at all events, that admiration supposes a scale of values. We give marks to actions, and the lower values go to the lower egotism."

"What makes us do that?"

"Ah! what does? Do you remember what we said about Evolution culminating in Mind?"

"That such a miracle could not happen if there were not a spiritual principle in the world? . . ."

"Precisely. In the same way there could be no scale of values in our reason if we did not possess a spiritual light showing us what is higher and what is lower. Kant and Newman build their belief in God on the existence of that light. All the time God, or the Spirit, wants us to rise above Matter constantly dragging us down. Morals is, according to the language which people adopt, either the supreme stage of evolution, or the voice of God speaking to our conscience."

"Do I need to believe in free will if I am to believe in morals?"

"How jauntily you throw this question in! Free will cannot be discussed as if it were a little side issue; you recall to me Madame de Staël asking Fichte to explain his philosophy to her while he sipped his coffee. Free Will! Do you still know what we are discussing and how far we have gone in our discussion?"

"I think I do. Man has been looking at the Universe, now he is looking at himself. He has found that he is spiritual, or partly so, and he hopes he is immortal; now he wants to hear whether or not he is morally free, for all we have found about morals will be useless if free will is a delusion."

"Marvellous! You certainly do know what we are talking about and that is no mean achievement when the topics are something else than mere business or trivial arrangements for the day."

"It all depends upon how interesting one finds a

discussion. I am keenly interested in free will. I have always been. Here's your man looking at the universe and at himself, isn't he?"

"Go ahead!"

"Easy enough. The case for determinism is as clear as daylight. My soul being associated with its body, that is to say matter, is limited by its material prison, of course. With a certain brow a man is intelligent, with a receding forehead he is stupid. Even if he is intelligent, he cannot be brilliant when he has a headache. So he is limited, predetermined by his material part. Now, just as my soul is limited by my bodily conditions, my activity is limited by the Universe in which I am plunged, is it not?"

"Unquestionably. You are terse and luminous."

"Easy enough, I tell you. When the day is too warm, I feel limp, body and soul; if it is wintry, I am numbed and unhappy. The universe about me, my surroundings have to be favorable. If I am poor and live on an out-of-the-way farm in Tennessee, I shall get little education. If I am well off, in New York or Boston, college will be at hand, refined company will be the natural thing: I shall be an educated, travelled person and my clever talk will delight the fortunate people who will move in my sphere."

"Was Lincoln a rich young New Yorker?"

"No, he was not, but he was a Kentuckian genius. What he lost in environment was made up for by what he possessed in his own right. The same with Shakespeare. A man is first the result of his individual components, material as well as spiritual, and, second, he is the result of circumstances which he cannot control. Therefore, he is determined on all

sides. If he were not—listen to this—he would be God."

"Do you like the idea of being imprisoned like that?"

"No, but I like logic and I would rather be uncomfortable than foolish."

"Heroic. But perhaps you need not be a hero. I do not believe in such iron determinism as that which your logic describes."

"Can you, are you free, to model like Michelangelo or write like Milton?"

"I might answer like the man who, being asked if he could play the violin, replied he had never tried and therefore could not tell. But a Scot's answer may give more food to your logic. Here it is: could not Milton have written *Paradise Lost* as poorly as he wrote *Paradise Regained?* Milton was not always at his best; the *Penseroso,* for instance, could be written by many a versifying sophomore."

"You mean that if I have a dollar I am free to spend only five cents, but I doubt if that applies to a poet. When Milton's inspiration was strong it produced Paradise Lost; *when it was feeble* Paradise Regained *turned out feeble. Conditions, as usual, determined the result, and it might have been predicted in advance."*

"Do you know what you are doing all the time?"

"Trying to reason logically."

"The very reverse. I speak of free will and you think of capacity. Nothing can be more illogical. A plain case of *ignoratio elenchi.* My freedom is not limited by my capacity. I cannot swim a hundred miles or, like nimble Attila, jump eight horses, but if I could, probably I would. If I make three thousand a year I cannot live as if I were making ten thousand, but I do not feel my liberty limited by my capacity. If I have two hundred dollars left I can spend them on a trip to Canada or on a set of the *Britannica,* as I please."

"You think you can."

"I am not sure of that, but if I think I can I do not feel hampered in my action, do I?"

"Aren't we hair-splitting?"

"You certainly are. You may even be quibbling. Let us be talking honest psychology. Haven't you been conscious many times of modifications of your own ideal taking place in your soul under the influence of your own thoughts?"

"Wanting to live upstairs, as you call it, instead of downstairs? Why! yes! I want to do good even when I do evil, and that fight will go on as long as I am not delivered out of the body of this death. It's my environment, flesh and world, that weighs me down. But my mind dictates differently and I am sorry or ashamed when I disobey its orders."

"Ah! here is the crux. In the first place our mind dictates differently from our flesh. Do you think that that could go on endlessly, as it does, if we never had our choice? Do you think that, through the thousands of years of his existence on earth, man could have been a mere toy, a puppet, and yet retain that exalted idea of good compared with evil, of nobility compared with mediocrity? Surely if this ideal were only a mirage, it would, long ago, have been obscured by solid facts."

"I admit that. I know that if I tell a reformed drunkard that his free will is only a dream, and if I

happen to convince him, the first thing he will do will be to go and get drunk."

"Of course, he will. And perhaps, for the first time in his life, he will neither be ashamed nor sorry. Being ashamed and sorry is the second thing that proves our moral freedom. Those uncomfortable feelings would certainly have vanished from a world in which everything was pre-determined like the motion of a clock."

"Unless the feelings themselves were pre-determined, perhaps."

"You know you can repeat those words, be pre-determined to repeat them, till doomsday. This means that, till doomsday, you would be begging the question. People do that all the time when they discuss free will. They, first of all, welcome all the arguments against free will, and to all arguments in favor of free will they answer: I can only be myself and not another; I cannot shake myself free from circumstances. That is why this old debate would seem bound to go on indefinitely were it not for a momentous change which has lately happened in physics. Have you heard of Professor Compton?"

"Just the name."

"Not enough! However, the doctrine is what counts. For a time, at least, it must silence classical determinism. Like all modern physicists Professor Compton has studied the behavior of atoms. What does he find? That atoms are freaks: that you never can foresee what they are going to do. In other words they are not pre-determined. If matter is not pre-determined why should spirit be?"

"Yes, but this is Science again. If I were not already convinced, science would not convince me."

"What convinces you, then?"

"What you said about the survival of my inner light in a world which ought to have extinguished it long ago: that *is convincing."*

"You feel, don't you, that the same Spirit, at work in the Universe, is also working in our Mind and Will. The still small voice is His."

"Yes, if I had absolutely no choice I should never know shame or remorse."

"You put it in a nutshell. Morals is built on that certainty. And if it failed us, the world would be uninhabitable, for appetites would rule it while beauty would desert it."

"I am glad you see Morals as a source of beauty. The word moral is not absolutely fascinating to modern ears."

"I know. It is gradually getting to resemble the word righteous which has long had a red nose, and delivers itself of platitudes through it. But, for all that, morals is not preaching, it is beauty of a rare kind. What the world has produced that has a right to the names of nobility or distinction is summed up as moral beauty. Really great men, benefactors—not rulers—of mankind, wise or sublimely kind men and women, give us the impression of beauty far more than many artists can. They are the connecting link between the lovers of abstract truth and the lovers of beautiful expression."

CONCLUSION

These are the chief problems of philosophy. In such a brief summary as the foregoing they can only be listed, but their mere enumeration may be enough to start the reader on a course of meditation as long as his life.

Some of these problems—for instance, the discussion of our cognitive possibilities—are frankly technical and, although all philosophers have faced them, they may be left to professionals.

On the contrary, other questions cannot but strike us by their immediate practicality. It only takes a moment's reflection to feel sure that a person who believes in free will and responsibility is less likely to become a criminal than another person who has no such certainty.

Most questions studied by philosophy, however, are neither purely technical nor obviously connected with our everyday life: they are speculative. Many people will be inclined to call them unpractical; but what is speculative is not necessarily useless in daily life. The discussion of the nature of matter at first sight is entirely speculative, interesting only to the physicist or the metaphysician. Yet, by one of its aspects it influences our belief or disbelief in the existence of God. Again the discussion of the existence of God, which, to most of us, brought up in a more or less religious atmosphere, appears as so vital, may seem speculative to a man who has grown up in unreligious surroundings: to him God is only an explanation of the universe.

The thinking of most people is limited to a narrow circle of immediate interests which they call practical life. Whatever is outside that circle they are inclined to brand as superfluous. The figures and data of geology and palæontology strike them as fanciful and of no earthly use. It will never cross their minds, when they see an apple and a pear on their table, to ask themselves at what stage of evolution these fruits had a common ancestor. The very notion of transformism seems to them unreal and uncomfortable. They banish it from their thoughts. Yet it is precisely the meditation upon the great speculative questions concerning man and the universe which, of its own nature, produces culture. We read half a page of a book, we listen for two minutes to a speech, it is enough to enable us to say whether the person who writes or speaks has that peculiar turn of mind or not. Culture is intellectual sympathy; mere practical pursuits, even of an intellectual character, can never produce it.

But wherever it exists, we know we are on the higher levels. No man has been interested in the explanation of his own existence and mind without the reflection of such thoughts appearing on his face in the nobility of his expression. Anxiety about those great issues is the evidence of the presence of God in us. No man who is conscious of it and acts in consequence can ever be low, or even trivial, or ordinary: the divine spark once active in him will not let him be a prey again to his material nature.

That is why philosophy, really worth the name, is not a specialty like philology. It should not be studied in what is generally regarded as a purely scientific spirit. Above all it should never be studied that we may brag about our acquaintance with it. The True should be sought for its own sake. Sometimes, during our quest, we shall be conscious of being in a semi-poetic, semi-devotional condition. That is the perfect philosophical mood. Its effect is at once to elevate us and make our intellectual faculties superior to themselves. But what matters is the altitude which we feel we have reached.

PART TWO

PULCHRUM

THE BEAUTIFUL

INTRODUCTORY NOTE

Is there a more powerful magnet than the beautiful, a more irresistible notion than that of beauty, an easier method of rising above the ordinary than a preference for what ravishes us?

Yet, we all have an uncomfortable sensation that we do not, cannot give in to that attraction, without a vague fear of insufficiently responding to it. How can we account for that contradiction?

Though so recent in the world, mankind has been analyzing too much. It has taught itself hair-splitting under pretence of attaining to full comprehension. The result has been what it always is: subtlety has disturbed simplicity without succeeding in satisfying itself. There is a veil of words even over nature, and the first thing to recall before investigating the rôle of beauty in our world and life is that beauty means primarily what seems beautiful to *us*.

INTRODUCTORY NOTE

Is there a more powerful magnet than the beautiful, a more irresistible notion than that of beauty, an easier method of rising above the ordinary than a preference for what ravishes us?

Yet we all have an uncomfortable sensation that we do not, cannot give in to that attraction without a vague fear of instinctively responding to it. How can we account for this contradiction?

Though so recent in the world, mankind has been multiplying [illegible]. It has taught itself hair-splitting under pretence of attaining to full self-liberation. The result has been that it always is [illegible] and disturbed simplicity without succeeding in satisfying itself. There is a veil of words over nature, and the first thing to recall before investigating the [illegible] in our world and life is that beauty [illegible] primarily what seems beautiful to us.

CHAPTER I

The Beautiful in Our Life

THERE is not a single human being who does not use, several times a day, the words "beautiful" or "not beautiful". Hardly an hour of our life glides by without giving us a chance of experiencing the delight of beauty: a face, an expression, an intonation, a mere gesture will cause us inwardly to note the warming presence of charm. We look absent-mindedly through the car-window as our train frees itself from a tunnel in West Pennsylvania; suddenly a smile of a peculiar quality steals over our face as, on the other side of the river, an assemblage of crags and trees appears, so perfect that it seems improbable. The light over the octagonal top of some New York downtown building at sunset does something to it which, even in their hurry, the crowds down below have to notice. A strain of music from a church, a picture in a dealer's window, a Chinese vase on a friend's table, an immense variety of chance combinations of line and color, or sounds, will produce the same effect: we become conscious of something above and apart which we cannot and will not disregard and which even anxiety finds a moment to greet.

What is it? What do we call that effect? A pleasure, no doubt, but a pleasure of such quality that we prefer to name it a joy; an admixture of appreciation and emotion which recalls pure intellection, but is nearer to us, goes home to us more naturally than any abstraction ever can.

When we seek that kind of pleasure, instead of merely welcoming it, a habit is soon formed; we become fastidious, and a sort of protective zone around us affects all our perceptions.

In the case of exceptionally sensitive—often also particularly gifted—people, contact with beauty becomes an hourly necessity to which everything else is sacrificed. Mere preference develops into a worship, and a whole life is transformed by it. Frequently the man thus affected combines manual deftness with rapidity of apprehension, and seldom resists the impulse to reproduce the beauty which enchants him: we call him an artist and see him in the same perspective with beauty itself. In a certain degree such people are magicians whose skill with words, sounds, forms or colors delights as well as it amazes us.

But they are also interpreters, of beauty first, of their own art afterwards, and most men and women similarly interested eagerly seek to commune with them. It is not merely their technical capacity that gives us pleasure. Anybody with a musical training can form a correct idea of a great pianist's talent from a record, but unless he can see that artist, once at least, in communication with his instrument and his audience he feels he misses a vastly important element of appreciation. This means that every real artist has his own magnetism which is an independent source of delight to us.

Many people want even more than that. They are not satisfied until they have made the personal acquaintance of the man who has thus charmed them. Sometimes their motives are not as disinterested as they should be, and their intrusion, promptly appearing in its true character, brings its own punishment. Sometimes such people are actuated by tendencies and wishes which all artists respect, and many noble friendships have been formed in that way.

Artists do not always know how to explain themselves: they are apt to be taciturn when they are not loquacious, and their language often is so technical as to be unintelligible. But most people who approach them never doubt that if they had missed that chance something invaluable would be absent from their life. I shall revert to this in another chapter.

When Jean-Jacques Rousseau, footsore and weary but full of expectation, reached for the first time the vicinity of Paris, he was disappointed, as many visitors have been after him. The long suburban street which he followed to the Barrière d'Italie screened the country from him and had no beauty to offer. Even the modernism of those days was soulless. It was only when he had extricated himself from the sordidness of the tanners' quarter on the malodorous banks of the Bièvre, that the young traveller descried, over the walled-in solitude of vast convent-gardens, the domes and towers he had been so long dreaming of. Then his soul revived, and, from that day, no matter how often he left Paris in anger or disgust, an irresistible attraction always brought him back there.

Imagine our life without beauty. What it is with beauty we ought to marvel at more often than we do.

CHAPTER II

What Is Beauty?

WHAT Beauty is all philosophers want, of course, to know. What is the psychology of esthetics? What is the share of the senses, and what is the share of the understanding in the perception, or the construction, of beauty? Above all what is the essence of beauty considered apart from its effect upon us? What makes it? Is it not divine, and what do we mean by saying that it is? All those questions tease the philosophical mind perhaps even more than the controversies about our cognitive faculties. Mathematicians have a curious affinity with poets, while poets and artists test and refine their technique till it finally appears to be nearer metaphysics than art.

But what about the answers to the question, what is beauty? They all open up vistas either in the sensuous or the metaphysical direction, but they never seem complete, they never satisfy. When our children ask us, as they invariably do, why this or that is beautiful and what makes it so, we are so embarrassed that our embarrassment makes us sincere. Our silence is one of the greatest surprises of the young. When they hear us differ about the beauty of some household object which to them seems beautiful from the very exaggeration in shape or color which gives us pause, they receive their first lesson in scepticism. A few years later they begin to look at art-magazines. They can hardly open one, they can hardly read the legend of a single picture without being given to understand that, however famous a work of art may be, its beauty can be or has been actually questioned. The past few generations have had to learn that lesson about such men as Turner, Delacroix, Corot or Monet. The results are well known: with the weak it is passivity, with the forward it is superficiality or pretence, with the sincere it is anxiety.

What should we do with regard to questions which have an immediate bearing upon our intellectual health and eventually react even on our ethical attitude?

There ought to be in every home a simple but comparatively complete History of Art which should give children a foundation of security. They cannot go through such a book without a certainty that however divergent or even contradictory the characteristics of works of art may be, admiration is unanimous about thousands of them. Eschylus and Euripides, Michelangelo and Raphael, Blake and Watteau, may not have a single point in common, but they are all admitted to have added to our enjoyment and comprehension of beauty. Therefore we can have the certitude that genius, when universally recognized, *makes beauty*. We can also be sure that when we study masterpieces we cannot be swerving from the line leading straight to the beautiful. In fact, whoever does that, whether in literature or in art, inevitably shows the superiority which we call culture.

But, neither in literature nor in art can we concentrate exclusively on the classics. We daily hear about the books, plays, music or painting of the day. Should we ignore the vast production which each season accumulates before our eyes? Evidently not, unless a special form of genius compels us to adopt such a decisive attitude. We must take cognizance of contemporary art. In what spirit? An admixture of sympathy and guardedness will be wisdom. When Cubism appeared there was an immense outcry against its evident charlatanry. There was also, on the part of a small minority, a disdainful assurance that the outcry was the familiar protest of philistinism. Whereupon not a few sincere people did not know what to think and waited in painful uncertainty till their minds were made up. What ought they to have done? The first thing should have been courageous sincerity: not pretend to understand when a handful of purple ribbons was entitled: *Portrait of a Bishop;* not pretend that Cubist manifestoes were intelligible; not give oneself airs of any kind. But there was no risk in saying that Cubists showed the imagination of Mexican Indians in playing with geometrical lines, or that the accidental oppositions of tones which women sometimes admire in the silks in their work-boxes were equally arresting on those canvases. That much could have been safely said, and it was also safe to say that few men of any school could plagiarize even the craziest Picasso. People who were resolved to limit their judgments to their impressions did say those things when Cubism appeared, and after twenty years, what they said is still the verdict of moderate criticism about that defunct school.

On the other hand, violent abuse has, for the last forty years, been poured on the manner of Cabanel, Bouguereau and the other so-called *pompiers* of the same period. Everything about them, their plastic preferences, their coloring, their emotional appeal, is declared false, unreal and only destined for people equally superficial and artificial. Quite so, but why not add that Cabanel and Bouguereau knew at least how to draw, which has become an extremely rare accomplishment now-a-days, and that, in the special light of the atelier, they even knew how to paint, knew how to select their colors and were virtuosi with the brush?

"A virtuoso is not an artist."

"Not always, but he is a virtuoso, which most artists are secretly praying to become, and perhaps with a little luck, perhaps with a little ill-luck, the virtuoso might have had the artistic revelation. Pope, in a place or two, writes like Shelley."

We have to grade artists according to their ideals, of course, but it is only fair to judge them also according to the correspondence between their particular ambitions and their actual achievements. When I read, over the signature of one of their admirers, that modern French architects must be judged not by what they build but what they write, I conclude that my old aversion to those gentlemen's productions is well-founded: those so-called artists are theorists but not artists. But when I find that Cabanel and Bouguereau's ambition was merely to be the Carlo Dolcis of the nineteenth century, I have to admit that they made a success where the architects failed: their gift may not have been of a rare order, it was a gift all the same.

So much for the attitude we should adopt in view of the endless controversies concerning the beautiful and its degrees. It is visibly the manifestation of prudence rather than of daring. But such a state of mind does not seem likely ever to lead us to a definition of beauty, and can we do without such a definition?

All the great philosophers have given their own definition of beauty. This is evident proof that even powerful minds are not satisfied with each other's views, and, once more, the door is opened to scepticism. But it does not follow, from the fact that even philosophical genius cannot give a definition of beauty, that there is the least uncertainty concerning beauty. A glance at Plato's *Phaedrus* or at his *Convivium* will promptly convince you that you can trust your own experience. Only beauty is so multiform and elusive that a formula can never imprison it.

Does it pay to look for the formula? It always pays to strive to bring as many data as possible into the unity of as comprehensive a statement as possible. All artists do it. You see them acting as if they were mere artisans, or exclusively preoccupied with technical methods, intended to produce superior effects but still of a material order: you are tempted to imagine that their minds are concentrated upon those results and on nothing higher, but this is a mistake. No matter how uneducated some of those artists may be, the everlasting necessity for them to discriminate between what is beautiful and what is less so keeps their minds interested in the essence of beauty. In time most of them build up for themselves a system of esthetics which they may not be eloquent enough to describe but about which, when cross-examined, you never see them hesitate. Their emotions all tend to become intellectual, that is to say, they endlessly perfect their culture.

We have not the same chances to rise from experience to metaphysics, but we shall prove gainers if, while pursuing beauty, as we all do, we bear in mind some one of the more famous definitions of beauty. Kant's formula "*The beautiful is a finality without a purpose*" is thin in comparison with his general views on art and will soon be exhausted. But nobody, artist or not, who will play with the much older Platonist definition: "*Beauty is the splendor of truth*" long enough to go beyond its apparent obviousness, will fail to notice how marvellously it will grow upon him. Keats was ravished by it.

CHAPTER III

Effects of Beauty

Some of them have already been hinted at in Chapter I of this Part II. But there are more.

The natural effect of beauty is to raise us up, without any sensation of effort, to our higher level. We cannot admire a great natural scene, a sunset, an exceptionally striking seascape, a storm, without at once feeling remote from our personal littlenesses. Gossip, or the expression of petty grievances, is impossible to people while visiting the Parthenon, for instance, or the Lincoln Memorial. We cannot lay down one of the great books and proceed to think our smaller thoughts. In the same way we feel sure that the tone of conversation must inevitably rise in a home where only the best radio music is admitted.

You know the popular picture by Giorgione entitled the *Concert*. A monk is playing the organ. A man and a woman are listening to him before starting to accompany his music. The organist has been fingering the keys for some time. He turns his very Italian face, lighted up by large expressive eyes, from the keyboard, and he looks at his companions. The whole picture has been conceived to give that glance its full significance which is perfectly familiar to us. The organist loves his music, but he has not, so far, entered the stage in which he will be so overwhelmed by it that he will forget there are people at his elbow. He is absorbed both by the beauty of what he is playing and by what he knows must be the echoes of that music in the souls of his companions. The overtones resulting from this combination are what Giorgione has had the audacity to paint and has succeeded in painting. Even a child can tell that this organist is in a mental condition into which nothing, except nobility, can enter: the artist's psychology, rich and complicated as it may be, is however perfectly clear.

Why is it that, after giving such a masterpiece the attention to which it has a right, we not only feel well above our ordinary but are conscious of a keen desire to give the world of our best? A fleeting esthetic sensation may not be enough to produce that effect, but every time we have been rebaptized in beauty we want our self-improvement to be contagious, productive and generous. You walk absentmindedly into the Metropolitan Museum, and after some aimless rambling you find yourself in rooms XX and XXI which happened to be closed the last time you were in the Museum. The rarest Corots, the rarest Courbets are there, with a sprinkling of unique Manets, Monets and Cézannes. Not one trivial choice, everything unexpected, yet, somehow, longed for. Finally you become engrossed by two flower-pieces, rarer than all the rest, by Courbet and Degas. The whole room begins to act upon you as if it were one picture. You smile, you forget your worries. You enter into the general harmony. A moment comes when the whole thing is so entrancing that you cannot bear it any longer. You walk out of the room, but in a few moments, the prodigy of prodigies, the radiant *Cardinal* by El Greco is before you, outshining everything else for you, and working on your sensibility as triumphantly, almost as mercilessly, as the *Hungarian March* of Berlioz sometimes does.

Is it surprising that when you are again in the Avenue, the sky, the Park are no longer what they were when you walked in? But why, coupled with a shrinking from all possible vulgarity, do you also feel the urgent necessity to make the most of your smallest chances, at every hour, every minute? The answer is easy. Beyond the canvases you have projected your soul into the souls of the artists, and their devotion to something beyond beauty, beyond ideal, the something which to them is God, has overcome your own consciousness. We can safely grade artistic works by that effect.

All around us, after such an experience, surges the modern world with its machines, its standardization and power. Yet we know we can resist it as if it had only the strength of a child. The true way, of course, is to give it the sympathy to which it has a right, viz., the kind of sympathy which southern people give to their colored servants. The machine is useful, sometimes admirable. Let the specialist multiply his inventions as much as he can. The artist will be with him. Sometimes, when the artist's name is Leonardo da Vinci, he will even help him. But he will never bow to the machine itself. He will use it to be freer, to secure more time and more agility, in a word to be more at liberty to enjoy what is *not* the machine.

That is what beauty does for us.

CHAPTER IV

Paradox of the Artist

IF ART is so naturally elevating, why is it that the artist has not the reputation of being over-moral? For, in spite of the general laxity, there is a lingering prejudice against the artist as a man who frequently does not submit to the rules of decent society and will not even see that hypocrisy is vice's homage to virtue. Many artists, most artists, I might say, are of bourgeois stock and, in consequence, know bourgeois families and are known to them. For three hundred years in Italy, for a hundred and fifty years in France, for at least fifty years in Anglo-Saxon countries, artists have been sought by connoisseurs and are more and more treated by them on a footing of equality. People no longer entertain any doubt that a painter's family, as well as an actor's family, is often older-fashioned than a stockbroker's might be. Yet, the majority of our contemporaries still look down upon artists—the vague community of artists—as morally inferior. They respect physicians whose 'prentice years were never marked by austerity, but they do not respect artists. There are curious nuances in their mistrust of artistic morality: they are more on their guard against the painter than against the sculptor, they trust the writer less than the musician, and they regard the architect as just one of themselves.

Prejudices subsist in people's imagination long after they have been destroyed by their experience: society is full of such survivals. There is little doubt but the prejudice against artists goes back to the Renaissance and to the introduction of the living model into studios. One of the great shocks that the pietism of the sixteenth century received in Rome came from the freedom with which the Popes would drop in upon artists at their work. La Bruyère is right in pointing out that some minds are obsessed by only one kind of sin, that is to say, harbor only one kind of preoccupation.

But this is not all. Everybody knows the power of conformism, especially in Anglo-Saxon countries. Freedom—which one is supposed to prefer to life itself—does not extend to hats, beards, costumes, habitations or even location. You are almost an expatriate if you live in a quarter where "nice" people do not live. Moreover the artist is not regarded as doing real work: that can only be done at an office. The money he makes is not called a salary and the legislation brands it as an "unearned income". The artist may be a careful man, cherishing for the bank a reverence bordering on awe, he is still accused of being a bohemian with no sense of credit and debit, no foresight, and no wish for the only kind of success that counts. Many people bow to Rubens because he, at all events, possessed a good home, had secured a large income and was visited by real people.

There are two things which philistinism will never take into account in its judgment of artists: one is the inevitable predominance of one set of faculties in their mentality, the lopsidedness which must exist in a Whitman as it does in a Newton; the other is the heroic sincerity which not only characterizes but makes the real artist. The ignorance of the thing called success which compelled Michelangelo to live, to his dying day, the life of an ascetic; the renunciation by Rembrandt of the popularity which had made him a rich man, simply because he insisted on painting what his genius told him, and not what his buyers wanted him, to paint, are things which are as much beyond average appreciation as saintliness itself. To the great artist they are natural: he is as superior morally as he is professionally exceptional.

"But what about the rank and file of artists? Would you also say that they are morally superior?"

Most undoubtedly if you will remember the true meaning of the word moral, which is a preference for the spiritual instead of the material, and if you will also remember that not every painter, sculptor, poet, or musician is an artist. The cult of the nineteenth century for talent has produced an immense desire for it which, in its turn, has given rise to innumerable ambitions not always accompanied by a gift. There are in Paris alone between four and five thousand painters. How many will be remembered in fifty years? Hardly one in a hundred. The rest are men and women who might have adopted, ought to have adopted, another profession. Unfortunately it is infinitely easier to paint or model than the public suspects: so, it is not difficult for people fascinated by the word artist to set up as painters or sculptors and act as if they actually were the favorites of the Muse.

However, here as in everything else, the usual psychological laws operate. Insincerity will make these so-called artists more and more insincere: they will become the kind on whom the grocer around the corner does well to keep his watchful eye. But if, on the contrary, there are enough possibilities in the would-be artist to give him an honest hope of producing beauty, that certainty, coupled with association with superior people, will result in the real artist's brave attitude before life. Sometimes talent of an exceptional order will be found to be dominant in a soul which otherwise might belong to a distinctly unmoral or immoral person. Then devotion to beauty will blossom out in its usual fascinating way, but it will not prevent the artist from occasionally acting as a scoundrel. Bernard Shaw, whose literary weakness is a perpetual dread of seeming conventional, has chosen, in *The Doctor's Dilemma*, to present to us an artist of that mixed kind. His Dubedat is a contemptible rascal. But every time the artist in him asserts himself he becomes lovable and enviable. Finally the dramatist kills him on the stage and, however inclined he may have been to avoid the least suspicion of conventionality, he feels he cannot show us an artist dying in an ignoble manner and Dubedat dies bravely.

Whether natural or acquired, devotion to beauty cannot but produce an attitude we respect, even when the artist imagines that he has a right to everybody else's collaboration, that is to say money, even when he acts as if he actually had that right. For he will be found to sacrifice his comfort, his peace, his very ambition to his art. And whoever is equal to such a sacrifice is above mediocrity. That capacity for self-denial is the source of the artist's simplicity, of his childlike disinterestedness and beautiful certainty that other people can also be above their own petty interests. Artists are proverbially kind. They are the only people, socially superior to the working-classes, who possess the virtues of the working-classes. Their faith is touching, and even when their religion happens to be tinged with their peculiarities, it is apt to give them a much more Christ-like ideal than the Pharisees who look down upon them will ever possess. As a matter of fact, when they are told that their very vocation makes them work with the Spirit and for the Spirit, their philosophy causes them to appear far superior to the Monist who regards the word spiritual as a personal insult.

CHAPTER V

Enjoyment of Beauty Is Natural to All

Who can doubt it? Even the uneducated will admire a natural scene or be sensitive to the color of the day or to the character of the season. The remarks of the rudest peasant about the weather have an esthetic side. As for the capacity of simple people to notice the essentials of artistic beauty, it is a commonplace. Rough soldiers rambling in the streets of an old European town will give the cathedral its due, even if it shows the dilapidation which common men seldom forgive.

You may say that this apparent appreciation is acquired: where we admire receptivity we should only see imitation. It is true that the stock in trade of popular admiration is limited to a few adjectives, everlastingly the same, and the letters of so-called unsophisticated people are full of clichés. But long before the apparition of adjectives and clichés primitive man must have expressed his interest in natural beauty: the expression may have consisted merely of exclamations, gestures, or emphatic silence, but it was a beginning.

What is true of primitives is also noticeable in children. Their first impressions of what we call nature are, of course, indistinct and largely tactile; they prefer summer-days because of the caress of the heat, they love the pattering of a shower, the lightness of the first flurry of snow, and they catch the frolicsomeness of the wind exactly as kittens do. But they are not slow in adding conscious reflection to those sensations. I remember a little fellow of four who, on warm afternoons, would listen delightedly to the soft warbling of other children in the next garden. He had no idea that he was in a poetic state, but he was.

If there is something mysterious in human psychology it is the correspondence between the details of a landscape and our reaction to them. Yet even moderately gifted children early perceive that correspondence and perhaps wonder at it. They become initiated in the gradation of natural beauty much as primitive man must have been. Very young children are not conscious of anything like *mana*, or a mysterious presence, in some places rather than in others, but children under six notice it and are awed by it. Observe them, if they are apart from their company a while, in such a place as the Gorge of Vaucluse with its giant cliffs looking down on the mystic fountain, or in the sterner sections of the Grand Canyon: they are overpowered. In a grove of Celtic oaks they will be conscious of the eeriness which both attracted and terrified our druidical ancestors. There is a place described by Plato at the beginning of the *Republic:* visibly the philosopher is trying to convey the impression that this place, although not so formidable as a lonely forest or a mountain-gorge, was eerie: a child would feel this character quite as vividly as a man.

It takes more time and culture to attune one's soul to one of those landscapes apparently so like hundreds of others that at first they seem uninteresting. We all know of such which familiarity, instead of making contemptible, has rendered lovable. Gradually unsuspected harmonies between them and our own soul are discovered. We are apt to imagine that such a discovery only comes to well-read people who know what Amiel means when he says that a landscape is a state of consciousness, but it is not so. I once caught a shepherd, an extremely rough man whom I knew well, gazing at an indifferent expanse of wheat-fields and pasture-land at the end of which the spire of a village church was seen slanting in a sleepy attitude. "I like to look over there," the man said, to my surprise.

One more step, and observation will perceive the nuances which the hour or the season create with such lavishness in any bit of country, even within the narrow limits of a garden, and which give them what we rightly call their soul. When a man notices these, he also begins to look upon them as one of the chief sources of his pleasure. From that moment he will be likely to experiment upon them and to add to his pleasure by the well-known devices of interruption, variation or repetition. From that moment also he will be an artist, for one is not an artist only because of what one makes or says, but because of what one feels.

So, even the keenest psychological enjoyment is possible to all men in the presence of beauty.

Why is it then that so many people regard that kind of enjoyment as a sort of specialty? Why is it that when they hear it mentioned they feel inferior, once more, and try to be reconciled to their inferiority as they do in the case of social inequalities?

This disastrous phantasm is largely produced by another, which is the impossibility for anybody except a specialist in literature or art to express beauty. There are too many pictures and too many books: their presence leads the average man to imagine that if he cannot paint or write he can only enjoy what other people paint or write, but should never presume to feel or express anything personal. This deterrent, at the stage of civilization in which we are, has acquired a formidable power. Only country people well out of the reach of print are free from it.

The historian of literature who has his share in the spreading of this absurd notion ought to point out a fact which might help in exorcising it. There is no doubt that the expression of delight at natural beauty has been refined in the course of ages, in such a way that even an average person to-day is conscious of nuances which ancient poets never perceived. Loti, for instance, teaches us a multitude of sensations which Michelet, only forty years before, did not experience. Going backwards, Chateaubriand felt more things than his English predecessors; Cowper more than Milton; Milton more than Virgil or Homer. Yet we derive the same satisfaction from Homer's expression that we derive from the nuances perceived by all his successors down to Loti. And Loti, in his turn, will inevitably be left behind by some future writer as gifted as he was and having the advantage of his predecessor's experience. This shows us that only one thing is necessary to enjoy beauty in an eternal way, and that is sincerity.

Women who, less than men, are influenced by books also show more independence in their sensations. I noted with surprise and satisfaction once the tone in which an old aunt of mine, towards the end of a wet winter, spoke of "the black dampness of the garden." Innumerable other women have hit upon equally graphic phrases which professional writers would gladly treasure and set in good light in their books if they should occur to them.

So, the cult of beauty does not belong to the few but to the many, and technical ability has nothing to say to it. Painters or sculptors often envy the reactions of visitors who can boast of no manual dexterity but show as much impressionability as they themselves possess. I once went through the English galleries with a young Frenchman who had already given proofs of exceptional talent in the handling of pen and ink. To my amazement this so-called artist was passive before the most striking pieces and only noticed technical brilliance. He never exhibited either the emotion or the inquiring spirit which are the characteristics of the real artist. He had a talent but no soul.

CHAPTER VI

The Enjoyment of Art Possible to All

"Why not, seeing that the enjoyment of natural beauty is a pleasure and not an effort?"

"Ah! but nature does not play on me the tricks in which art evidently delights. Here's a piece of gray canvas: if Courbet toys with it a few hours it will be transformed into a face more alive than life itself; if Corot takes hold of it there will be a pond at early dawn with the morning mist hanging over it. This is a legerdemain much more extraordinary than producing a bouquet out of an empty hat. How can I admire the face or the misty pond without wondering how the conjurors brought them into existence?"

"Why! the trick is easy enough, at all events the directions for performing the trick are not difficult. You know that perspective gives depth to the Corot while lights and shades produce the relief in Courbet's face. You certainly know that the juxtaposition of pure tones results in light and . . ."

"I know nothing. I know that art critics who seem so satisfied with themselves give me the impression that even they know no more than I do. They have learned a language which I cannot master and they speak it to show me what fine fellows they are. Art is a mystery to them and it is not surprising that it is one to me."

"You are right, astonishingly right, about most art critics, and the artists who are not afraid of them, or do not kow-tow to them, would applaud what you say. The moment an art critic retires behind his smoke-screen of formulas *you* should retire into good-humored contempt for his little trick. However, do not be too absolute: there are some art critics who are perfectly intelligible, that is to say honest. Read those, and if you chance on Reynolds' *Discourses* or on Delacroix' *Diary* you will find that artists can write clearly about art and you will learn a lot. But why not just stand before a picture or a statue and merely ask yourself if you like or dislike it?"

"Because I have found, dozens of times, that when I do that I make mistakes of which I am ashamed. Somebody comes along and begins to make remarks which prove to me that what I like is not artistic, while what I am blaming are refinements which people, who know better, admire. Shall I tell you something? It is not so long ago that I used to admire chromos. Honestly admired and loved them. Gradually I found out that it is shameful to do so, as one should admire nothing below colored engravings. But I have also discovered that between a chromo and a colored engraving there's only the thickness of a word. Those things are puzzling."

"Don't tell me that you admired all chromos, simply because they were chromos. Industrial art can produce things which are much nearer art than machinery. The Plasse process, for instance. Some chromos are far superior to some colored engravings. That was the kind you loved. Or you enjoyed the subject and your imagination supplemented possible deficiencies in the treatment. The great principle . . . "

"Ah! the great principle . . . "

"Is this, Mr. Ironist: whatever we love, sincerely and honestly love, teaches us to love something higher in the artistic scale."

"Suppose I love, honestly love, as so many people do, detective stories . . ."

"Well, even that. If you enjoy Mr. Chesterton's detective stories for what in them is inevitably artistic, you will be enjoying not a detective story but the art of a writer. Everything depends on the angle under which we see objects. The Marquis de Mirabeau had a brother, nicknamed Mirabeau-Tonneau, who said of himself: 'In any other family I should be regarded as a genius and a knave: in my own I am regarded as perfectly honorable, but a fool'. A little art in a detective story can lead you on to the very best fiction, only you must look at the art."

"Perhaps I was wrong to introduce literature."

"Why? Art is art. But remember I have used the word love. You cannot say you love what you barely glance at and forget, even if you registered some approval of it. Loving a thing so as to be taught by it produces a very different attitude. When Charlotte Brontë was at school her classmates were amused to see her scrutinizing a common wood-cut which she would keep close to her shortsighted eyes sometimes for hours. But after that she would say wonderful things about it. That is the kind of enjoyment I mean."

"And your idea is that somebody who takes that

much pleasure in a wood-cut will later on be enraptured by an original Rembrandt etching."

"That is certainly what happened to poor patient Charlotte. The richer girls, when they went to London, spent their time in Regent Street. Charlotte Brontë, when at last she found herself there, went straight to the National Gallery and, in the Gallery, straight to the best things, and she thought herself in heaven. She had educated herself. We all can educate ourselves as she did."

"I suppose she knew all about the different schools and found her way through the National Gallery by just knowing who was which."

"Yes, she did. Her dread of being a provincial ignoramus taught her all that, as the same fear caused her brother Branwell to pore over a map of London till he knew the streets better than the natives. But Charlotte would have admired the Bellinis even if she had known nothing about the Venetians. I am afraid you are obsessed by the thought of imaginary prerequisites to enjoy such a simple thing as a picture."

"I don't mind the ancient schools. I can see the kinship between Luini and Leonardo, or the contrast between Michelangelo and Raphael. What is teasing and discouraging is what you read, even in the newspapers, about the contemporary schools of art, their theories, their manifestoes, their fights and their lingo."

"Do you think many works of those manifesto-makers will be in the Louvre or the Metropolitan Museum in a hundred years?"

"I can see them in a room by themselves as a chronological link between periods."

"I see. Not works of art but historical documents."

"That's what they are."

"That is indeed what they are and they could not be described better. But if you feel sure that those strange things are not works of art why do you bother about them? Are we not discussing the possibility of *enjoying* art?"

"Yes, certainly, enjoying art without feeling that perhaps one is missing something of the first importance."

"Ah! you are a true modern. Anxious, anxious. And let me tell you, anxious about nothing. Do you personally know any artists?"

"Not one!"

"Well, I know many. I respect them, love them, and I hope I understand them. Shall I tell you what I think is the kind of visitor they like to see in their studios?"

"Why, what you call 'enlightened connoisseurs', of course."

"A complete mistake. Your enlightened connoisseur is often a mere shadow of the not very substantial critic. He plants himself before a picture and what sort of encouragement or guidance does the artist get? Words, words, jargon and pretence. Artists hate the enlightened amateur, unless he buys. No, no, what they like is intelligent natural sympathy."

"Where does sympathy stop, and where does intelligence begin?"

"They go together. A real artist, remember, is more in love with his subject than with his presentment of it, no matter how much he may think of that. You know he spends days, weeks and months studying it. In time he becomes haunted by something which is the soul of this subject. The something that first arrested him and gave him his inspiration was that, but he was not conscious of it. He only realizes it when he is tantalized by that elusive appeal. He hardly ever succeeds in fathoming its fulness. Most artists are never, never satisfied with their work, but they remain under the spell which first persuaded them to begin it. Well, many people, not exceptionally gifted and entirely destitute of technical knowledge, do not look long at a work of art before they get at its soul. There they rejoin the artist, indeed begin where he left off. That is what he loves and is endlessly grateful for. That kind of admiration is a collaboration which, after all, real admiration always is."

"I think I see what you mean. I have known a poet who was grateful like that when you repeated some exceptionally haunting verse of his. He could no more exhaust the virtue of his own syllables than I could, but he was grateful to one for helping him."

"How right you are to think of poetry while speaking of art! Even so-called realistic artists are poets. All art should be enjoyed poetically, and neither words, nor the affiliations of schools, nor technical knowledge help in doing that."

"Probably the habit of going quickly through a gallery or a salon is responsible for keeping people from that poetic enjoyment and ultimately for creating obsessions. The real enemy of art is the drawing-room where you have to pretend, pretend you have seen, understood, and remembered. People, in order to pretend, rush through expositions. There is also a strange subtle fear even of pleasure. Enjoy-

ment seems to keep us from our work which is to look at more and more things, and we crush it. There is also the fear that, after a few minutes' delight, our appreciation may run dry and we may feel inferior as usual."

"I know all that. I have experienced that dread of running dry while reading."

"Have you? I have a remedy for that, a literary Roland for your artistic Oliver. Go through Hamlet *or* The Tempest, *enjoying only the familiar lines which have always delighted you: you will drink deep of them, even if you only give each one a minute or two, and you will not feel the running-dry obsession. Perhaps many people do this, instinctively or from experience. I feel sure Petrarch did it. Does he not begin a sonnet with:*

Passer mai solitario in alcun tetto?

I have no doubt he had been running through the imagery in the Psalms *as I do through Shakespeare, and the solitary sparrow staid in his mind."*

"Thanks. And what wonderful things are literature and art when you reflect that their supreme law is simply our own pleasure! Beauty is happiness, the kind of happiness about which we never feel doubtful."

CHAPTER VII

From Esthetic Impressions to Artistic Inclinations

We have just said that the enjoyment of beauty is natural to us. No less natural is the enjoyment of art. Why? Not only because the wonder of it enchants us, but because it helps us to become conscious of the artistic propensities which exist in all of us. Art results in more art.

"But I do not produce anything artistic!"

"You mean you build no cathedrals, carve no capitals, paint no frescoes and do not play the organ. But you sometimes sing, which is an art; you can tell a story in a vivid manner, which is an art, and you can mimic people in a way which many comedians—artists by universal admission—might envy. Every man is an artist, and many who had never suspected it have become professionals overnight. I know a man who, one morning, began to etch, as he might have started being a vegetarian, and did remarkably well. A well-known sculptress began to model the first day she saw somebody else handling clay, and needed no apprenticeship. Taine, who had never written a verse, sat down at sixty and produced the famous sonnets on cats. Hundreds of people play the piano by ear and might have had their talent spoiled forever if they had had a teacher. The thing, as common parlance calls it, was in them, and I am always inclined to believe what the people of two generations ago used to say, viz., that each person has, dormant in him, a talent which is only waiting to be wakened up."

But there is no time to think of talent. We have to make a living and as, every ten years, the standard of living rises, every ten years our work grows harder. Also, as I said in a previous chapter, we are hypnotized and intimidated by the presence of an army of specialists, wrongly calling themselves experts, who speak of their own art as of a martyrdom and leave us wondering why we ever thought of it as a joy. You notice that many mothers do not tell the old stories to their children; it is because Mother Goose has been printed and reprinted a thousand times and because, every night, a bedtime story comes into the nursery over the radio. A tradition is stopped, in that way, while a phantasm is created or fortified.

Luckily while the mother loses the little chance she had to develop a gift as a story teller, children are not influenced, at least in their earliest years, by any such intimidation. They go on indulging the instinct which every now and then prompts them to sing and half-rhyme, instead of just telling, what has happened to them. They play at make-believe as their grandfather did, and love being terrified by their own imaginations. Few are those who being given a paint-box do not dream of the problems which keep artists awake: paint without an outline which does not exist in nature, paint the light, paint the night. Sometimes they ask their elders for help and information. If you tell them that what they are after is art, they think it a great joke, and show more sense than the Bourgeois Gentilhomme did when he was told that 'Nicole, I want my slippers' was prose, and repeated the sentence in delight because it was prose. The nearer people are to nature the more instinctive art seems to them. The canticles of the Hebrews were the natural outbursts of people whose poetry was the expression of their national life. The Corsican or Basque improvisers intrigue only strangers. The Orientals telling each other stories all night would feel cheated if they did not tell them. Only, listen to them with a certain air of puzzled admiration, or make notes of what they are saying and let them suspect that those notes are going into a book, you will at once make them conscious and their gift will suffer from the consciousness.

Everybody to-day knows the theories propounded to explain the artistic instinct, or seeks its earliest manifestations. They are chiefly useful in bringing us back to our most primitive stratum of consciousness and in setting in motion our only natural criticism. However it will not be amiss to investigate our nearness to such primitive arts as lyricism or music or the imitation of life. Whatever may strengthen our belief in the instinctiveness of art not only adds to our knowledge but helps to protect us against the artificiality of the contrary conception.

CHAPTER VIII

Lyricism and Music

Both lyricism and music are natural to us. They seem to be out of our reach because they have been made technical by generations of professionals, but they are so only in appearance, or because we do not dare to look at them closely.

All emotions attune us to a beginning of lyrical expression. Take up *Antigone* which you may think of as an old Greek play but which is in every line as modern as *Othello:* you will not have read fifty lines before you become aware that Antigone, like all princesses, speaks with the directness, simplicity and vehemence of a woman of the people, but there is in her phrasing and rhythm something winged constantly ready to soar upward. That something is a barely repressed lyricism, and when the chorus suddenly breaks out into its aerial stanzas they seem so natural that we feel like joining in.

The lyrical tendency is as perceptible in the language of many of our contemporaries as it is in Antigone's tirades. When high-strung people tell us about their woes, the injustice they have suffered, the nemesis which sometimes has followed it and the ultimate triumph of right, we expect a sudden interruption of the narrative and a soul-born exclamation introducing the comment of indignation or joy: that comment is invariably lyrical and often shows a tendency to be rhythmical as well.

Even when nobody is near to share in our emotion we seldom succeed in keeping it to ourselves. There is little doubt but the first man who, many centuries ago, saw a peacock displaying his rainbow to the solitude exclaimed and exclaimed till his delight found an expression far more intense than his everyday language. To-day when we happen to be in a similar state of mind we may be enjoined by the levelling-out thing called civilization to be as quiet as possible, but we gladly embark on the stream of our emotion and we float down with it as long as the current is strong enough to carry us. Then what do we do? Do we take up a novel or a volume of plays to provide us with a suitable transition from excitement back to humdrum uniformity? Certainly not. We ask Browning or Madame de Noailles, or a manuscript collection of poems of our own selection to prolong a mood which we have long learned not to waste.

The presence of those volumes on our shelves is not altogether good for us. If we did not know that they are within reach we might not feel satisfied till we had given our emotion some permanence, were it only in a one-line poem like those which seem so rich to the Japanese imagination. As it is, we are grateful to lyrical poets for giving our mind the accompaniment it needs: a melancholy rhythm if we are pensive, a brisker song if we feel happy.

You may say that only literary people, or people with a literary turn do this, and that average emotion is content with itself or finds insuperable obstacles to its own cultivation. Quite true, but people who write poetry force their way of feeling upon those who read it and eventually upon the whole community. For the cue given by the poet is taken up by the musician or by the painter, and you certainly know verses which have become popular, that is to say, influential, in that way. They result in the creation of a cultivated poetic state of mind the contagion of which we cannot escape. We can see nothing, experience nothing without a poetic echo answering the sensation, and we often seek the experience in order to waken up the echo.

Is it desirable to owe so much to literature and add so much to literature? Crabbed Cato said not, and the most poetic of philosophers, Plato, says no too. The idea of both men undoubtedly was that what may be pleasure for the individual will result, in the commonwealth, in a craving for pleasure, and republics should live on action and not on refined sensations. To-day we know only too well that the community, with its endless emphasis on co-operation, makes us active whether we will or not, and we would rather soften the individual than harden him. Civilization to us connotes progress, especially of an altruistic nature, but the notion of the artistic element is never far. That is why the idea that lyricism is an instinctive form of our self-expression should not cause much surprise.

Music is not different: it is only lyricalness in another form, and probably the two forms were born together of the same emotion. The well known cry of the Basque people on both sides of the Pyrenees, the *irinzina,* is a musical cry not quite so modulated as the Indian call but probably more primitive.

Let any circumstance warrant more emotion, the cry will be repeated and so modulated that it will have to be called music. The Basque improviser sings, so does the Basque *pelotari* who calls out the score of the game. Many primitives sing or whistle as instinctively as they speak. The medieval juggler who told his tale to the twang of an instrument no doubt was witness to an ancient and more than ancient tradition rather than to a development. The very word lyricism implies the use of a lyre. Worship has to sing, so has military action. No similarity, no doubt, between that singing expression of every-day sentiment and the recondite thing which we call music to-day. Yet, it seems probable that early music was more a transcript of the deeper agitation of the soul than an imitation of natural sounds, was nearer to the spirit of the *Pastoral Symphony* than to that of Massenet's unbearably literal *Alsatian Scenes.* It was sung sentiment as evidently as was Rameau's musical eloquence. On the whole it was pre-eminently lyrical.

Sensuous yet intellectual, indefinite yet speaking with absolute directness to our soul, music is certainly the language corresponding the most accurately to the medley of half-unconscious sensations with which primitive speech had to struggle. What poet would dare to retranslate Ravel's *Pavane for a Defunct Infanta* into even the most evanescent lyrics? The Escorial with its pomp and its tombs might be in the background, Spanish grandees might look on with the stern dignity filling El Greco's *Funeral of Orgaz,* monks might be chanting, ladies-in-waiting might be weeping and the nurse might be wailing, but no words would give, as Ravel's music does, beside all this, the impression of the barren grandeur of Castile, outside the royal monastery. Nothing could replace the flitting evocations which the heart-searching notes produce. Only the rhythm might—not convey to us that turmoil of sensations, but lead us to imagine that it does.

Only the rhythm. For lyrical rhythms act like music, that is to say, they would seem independent of the meaning of the syllables with which they are associated if we could ever dissociate that meaning from them. Mallarmé, Valéry and the other champions of "pure poetry" are entirely right when they ascribe the dominant evocative virtue to rhythm, that is to say when they admit that music and lyricism are only artificially distinguished one from the other. Read Poe's night-piece *To Helen*, every line of which can be understood by a child of ten, you will feel from the beginning that the real poem is not the one you read, but another, simultaneously whispered in a confidential repressed rhythm which gives it its full significance.

Perhaps this quality of the rhythm is even more perceptible in the following lines of the same poet, not so immediately intelligible as the poem *To Helen* and therefore nearer to the conceptions of Mallarmé or Valéry:

> Here once, through an alley Titanic
> Of cypress, I roamed with my Soul,
> Of cypress, with Psyche, my Soul.

Why are you arrested by these verses? Why will they inevitably recur to you? Why will you find yourself vaguely trying to remember a not very definite something and the something will turn out to be Poe's verses? The enchantment of the rhythm, acting identically like that of music, will be responsible.

The mistake of so-called "pure poetry" advocates is, as usual, an exaggeration. Because the rhythm is obviously more powerful than the words, these theorists conclude that it is best to attach as little sense as possible to their words. Hence the apparent disconnectedness of most of Valéry's poems; hence the strange fact that there exist two versions of Mallarmé's *L'Après-Midi d'un Faune,* one intelligible, the second laboriously transformed into a puzzle.

But it is difficult to abide by an exaggeration without running the danger of self-contradiction. One of the poets in whom pure poetry is declared to be at its best is Virgil, yet it is too obvious that the man who wrote the *Georgics,* great poet though he was, was nearer didacticism than he was to Mallarmé's conscious fancifulness. Another god of pure poetry-seekers is Racine, but these enthusiastic admirers seem to forget that Racine, for all that is exquisitely haunting in his dramatic poems, first wrote them in prose and certainly never thought of adding to them magical tags similar to Mallarmé's. He was and remains the incarnation of taste while Mallarmé and Valéry want too much that is rare, and in fact, lack measure.

Why is it that, poetry and music being natural to us, so many people are indifferent to music and show positive aversion to poetry? The reason is that those people are discouraged by too much music or poetry that is banal, or by too much that is, on the contrary, recondite. They run away from obviousness or from thickets of technicalities in which they only know too well that phantasms are lying in ambush. Who can blame them? But who will not pity them? They are the victims of a mistakenly conscientious notion that they have to understand everything, even the modernistic performances which they are sure to misunderstand. Strange that people should spend their whole lives without grasping the simple principle that in art what we like is what teaches us, and the fundamental fact that no great poet and no great musician has ever disappointed expectation.

CHAPTER IX

Life in Art—Drama and Fiction

Lyricism in words or in disciplined sounds is the natural outlet of human emotion when it finds nobody to whom it can be communicated, or when it is so overpowering that it has to use a medium superior to every-day language. Its naturalness is proved by its universality.

When human interest happens to be excited not in solitude but in company, other means of expression are ready at hand and immediately used. Nothing is more instinctive in us than imitation, or narration and description. The moment we are particularly impressed by any happening we feel the impulse to convey our impression of it through repetition, whether it be words or gestures, or a combination of both. The pantomime must have been the earlier expression, but even animals try to add a vocal emphasis to their gestures. Clearly the drama, or a thing acted, and the narration, or a thing told, have the same origin and can never be completely dissociated.

Literary history is apt to create incorrect impressions in its readers when it tells us that the sacred pantomime which, in all the mystery-rites, represented the life or death of the god, is the origin of the drama. These rites are of yesterday and, untold generations before them, the cave-man would act realistic dramas while his brother the artist was busy painting realistic figures on the rock. Dramatic and narrative literature flourish every day and all day, in the forest-cabin as well as in the king's palace.

Moreover, literary history itself corrects the impression which that stereotyped chapter of hers on the sacred drama inevitably creates. She tells us that Dickens positively acted his public readings, sometimes skipping a whole sentence when a gesture or two could replace it. We also read that the medieval juggler not only sang but acted his chanson. Finally, the new Homeric theory which sees in the *Iliad* and *Odyssey* collections of monologues destined to be acted as well as recited, may only be one more Homeric theory, but when you read the *Odyssey* by its light, you certainly avoid many of your former difficulties.

As usual the present state of literature misleads us. We see publishers and theatrical managers carrying on apparently different trades. We regard the cinema as drama but seldom as literature, and we are puzzled by the outside appearance of plays which do not seem things acted, or of novels which are something more than the word-transcript of an action. For instance, what about Mr. Shaw's dramas? What about Richardson's endless novels? The former are theories, the latter are a dissection of sentiment. Where is action?

Undoubtedly Mr. Shaw's book-plays deceive us. The introductions and stage-directions swell the play to twice its legitimate volume, and there is more philosophy than action in it. Also it is too evident that Mr. Shaw uses the play as an apologue and wants us to have no doubt that he does. But Mr. Shaw also knows his business as a dramatist. If you want the moral, here it is in the introduction; if you are too lazy to look for it there, here is a play. Were Mr. Shaw less conscious of the necessity of action, of action at all costs, which the ultra-practical Drama Schools of America indefatigably recommend, he could not indulge as he does in improbabilities. At the very moment he himself slinks on the stage and signifies to us as clearly as by words that he has found no *dénouement* to his plot but does not care, we transform him into the buffoon of the play and his originality adds to our amusement. Action is slower in his dialogues than in Racine's or Sophocles', each line of which corresponds to a step onwards, but Mr. Shaw's psychological reading of his characters is in immediate relation with their actions. His plays pretend sometimes not to be written for the stage, but it is only pretence.

As for Richardson's ten-volume novels, they may be long but they are not slow. The few readers they still find have never called their author a dull writer. Why? Because *Pamela* and *Clarissa* show as much action as *Moll Flanders,* only it is psychological action and we see the gestures of the soul instead of those of the body. But do we not find the same thing in *Hamlet,* which beats all modern plays for swiftness, and can be held up to the admiration of contemporary professionals as the typical modern drama?

"If both the novel and the drama are such spontaneous manifestations, why are they spoken of with so much admiration?"

You mean: why are there so few great plays or great novels? The list of immortal playwrights or novelists in any language is certainly short. I offended an American friend of mine, once, by referring to Mr. Galsworthy, whose talent I think I thoroughly appreciate, as "an author not quite of the first rank". "You make him appear a second-rate writer," expostulated my friend who was a literary man himself and ought to have known better the difference between "second-rate" and "not quite of the first rank". He understood, however, when I asked him whether he felt that, in two hundred years, Mr. Galsworthy would be rated the equal of Dickens or Fielding, but he never could be brought to a literary expression of his thought, for the average American is curiously shy of the language of criticism.

All the arts are simple in their origin and can be summed up in a few equally simple formulas, but the application of those formulas appears simple only to genius. We say that action, in both the narrative and the drama, should be predominant and that, when it is, the play moves swiftly. *Œdipus Rex,* for instance, seems to be a much shorter play than it really is. The consequence is that many narrators think their work perfect when it succeeds in avoiding the appearance of slowness. But one can produce that impression without attaining to human verity, and what is a play without that?

One of the chief attractions of the drama is the reproduction of men and women's idiosyncrasies, for we love them in life and enjoy them keenly when accidental excitement gives them emphasis. Hence all dramatists strive to recapture them. But while the greatest of them rise to the representation of character and create types, many are satisfied with hitting upon a few more or less striking but not deeply human traits. Most of even our famous contemporaries give us too much of modern man and not enough of man: they are satisfied with minor psychology. One degree lower, the author will limit his ambition to reproducing the familiar or trivial ways, the superficial mannerisms of his generation. How many plays owe their ephemeral success to technique and to a knowledge of current slang! How many have been indebted to the automobile, the airplane or the telephone! Sometimes to even less. I have seen an audience delighted every time the actress replaced "yes" by the gentle grunt which does duty for it in certain milieus.

Truth always gives us pleasure and it always teaches us a lesson. However there is, in dramatic literature, something even superior to that, which transforms a play into a poem and gives it an unsuspected virtue. We feel that extraordinary quality in the ancients, and we are conscious of it the moment we open Shakespeare or Racine. What that is it is not easy to say. It is not the verse—although we cannot imagine the great Shakespearean dramas entirely written in prose—for that magic is attached even to prose-scenes. Evidently the playwright has been conscious of his gift as an enchanter and, while going on with his action, he has applied his rhythmical power to it in a way which we cannot escape. It is not differently that, while reading *Waverley, Ivanhoe,* or *The Antiquary,* we feel that Sir Walter must have been an extremely attractive personality. Where a writer produces that combination of perfect technique, human interest and truth, and can add to it that supreme touch, the perfection of art has been attained.

Noble plays transform average actors into the depositaries of a great national, even a great human heritage. They work a similar transformation on the audience which enjoys them. The quality of the dramatic art in any country could safely be inferred from the remarks overheard at the door of a theatre. Once, after a performance of *Madame Butterfly* at the Chicago Opera-House, I heard a gentleman expressing his opinion that "this music might be excellent music, but the play was a vulgar play". How seldom can a human reaction of that kind be noted! Much rarer is a literary appreciation which the fear of "high-browism" would preclude even if the temptation to express it were actually felt. Most often the actress is pronounced clever or uninteresting without much effort at analysis, while the adjectives "slow" or "good" apply more to the evening than to the play. Such signs are not favorable.

CHAPTER X

The Arts of Design

THEY are: design, of course, architecture, sculpture and painting. Most people are deluded by the language into a belief that these are the real arts, that is to say, the only arts. We prefer calling a pianist a pianist rather than an artist. Beethoven is a composer, not an artist. Poets are only called artists by critics, and especially when their attention is concentrated on forms of a rare and exquisite nature: those of Poe, for instance, or Baudelaire.

Those tricks of the language are frequent, and we should be on our guard against them. All interpretative representation has a right to be called artistic and its author is an artist. If we were, in this connection, to be limited by usage, the only artist would be the illustrator or cartoonist, for the painter is a painter and the sculptor is a sculptor, but the illustrator is always called the artist.

Historians of civilization, therefore, are right in placing in a class apart the arts based on the use and combination of lines, and, design being the parent of them all, it is not amiss to call them by its name.

CHAPTER XI

Design

No PLASTIC art can exist without design. Architects, sculptors and painters all depend upon their portfolios. So does the village-carpenter. So did prehistoric man with his notes on bits of slate, and so do all gifted children whom we see trying any appealing combination of lines.

It is not easy to draw well. Try your hand at some exceedingly simple outline: a cigarette on the edge of a table, for instance: you will soon have to admit that you might take years to produce a drawing that would not disgust you. It is true that properly trained Mexican children have astonished New York by the mastery of their design. But critics did not sufficiently point out at the time that these young artists seemed, like their ancestors, to prefer grimacing models to beautiful ones, the faultlessness of which can be marred by an error of a hundredth of a line. It might have taken those children many more years merely to grasp the perfection of Raphael's design when, at barely nineteen, he was playing with the exquisite curves of his *Betrothal of the Virgin.*

Mastery in design can only be acquired by early training prolonged by life-long practice. This no great artist has ever allowed himself to neglect.

Rodin never let a day go by without producing miracles of drawing in his gossamer sinuous outlines. Bourdelle would get up at five every morning to save an hour for his drawing exercise. But one might make an endless list: our museums are rich in pencil or charcoal sketches which illustrious artists dashed off merely to keep their hand in. Some are famous. A few heads scattered over a sheet by Watteau rival his masterpieces. Everybody knows the portrait of Erasmus by Holbein at the Louvre. Few people study it without noticing the philosopher's sensitive hands. Holbein loved those hands, and it gives the unguided visitor rare pleasure to discover, in a faraway corridor, a careful study which the artist had made of them before painting the portrait.

All great painters have been proud of their design, and some have not been above *tours de force* to show their skill. The Italian phrase: *rotondo come l'O di Giotto* recalls the fact that the artist could use his O as a signature because it was inimitable. When Goya, aged and an exile, lived at Bordeaux, he would ask the people he met at the cafés there to drop three crumbs at random on a piece of paper, and however remote or awkwardly separated these might be, he never failed in drawing a figure with its head and hands where the crumbs had been. Ingres, dignified Monsieur Ingres, was such a swift draughtsman that his performances bordered on acrobatics.

Over against these prodigies, Corot is famous for the insufficiency of his design. Nothing is apparently so easy as to sketch a rheumatic apple-tree, every branch of which is crooked. As a matter of fact it is not easy and Corot could not do it. Yet he is a master of design in comparison with many artists who have come after him. The inadequacy of most of our contemporaries in that respect is notorious. They insist on painting, as some people insist on singing, without proper training, and the results are the eye-sores we know. The old saying: there never can be style in painting unless drawing predominates, is not only true, it is so rich in sense as to be well-nigh inexhaustible.

All that has been said above applies largely to drawing as subservient to the other arts, especially painting. But drawing is an art by itself which appeals to the psychologist, or to the imaginative as well as to the humorous artist, who have so much to say that they must say it quickly. Familiar examples abound. They are numerous in America where wit is plentiful, and where satire is generally so good-natured that one does not get tired of it. But it is when one goes back to the giants of the craft, Hogarth or Daumier, that one realizes what a keen eye and a quick hand in the service of truth at all costs can do with just pen and ink. And if one remembers that drawing can by simple processes be transformed into all the varieties of engraving, great vistas open for us in the long past of art. Dürer appears, and, shortly after him, Rembrandt, with his supreme excellence, sometimes his sublimity, radiating from ten-inch-square bits of copper-colored paper.

CHAPTER XII

Architecture

THE very name of this art sounds ample and dignified, ancient and venerable. There is also in it something recondite: a mathematical foundation difficult to obtain, a knowledge of unwieldy materials which only learned technique can conquer. Add that architecture, quite as much as painting, is given up to the debates of theorists, some buildings being declared by a few experts to be beautiful while everybody else thinks them ugly. The result is that we regard architecture as the business of states, cities, kings or rich communities, and stand rather in awe of it.

We may discuss our towns, comparing them with their neighbors or with foreign counterparts; we may be able to tell why we love the château unexpectedly discovered from its ha-ha or from a clearing in the wood; we can set the new church over against the old one; but almost invariably we lack confidence in our impressions, and we leave it to the specialist or to the prevalent fashion to plan our house for us.

This attitude is a legacy of the past. Till the fifteenth century in Italy, till the sixteenth in France, architecture did not concern private citizens. The homes of even the richest people in ancient Rome astonish us by their exiguity and unpretentiousness. Feudal towers, it is true, were added to a few mansions in Florence or Brescia, and there are two left in the older part of the Archives building in Paris, but such town-houses were exceptional: medieval towns like Siena, Carcassonne, or Salamanca were entirely subordinate to their monuments or to their military defence, their streets did not count. To us the rows of houses clinging like ivy to the cathedral, or the timid streets running for protection straight up to the castle are deeply touching. Substitute modern magnitude and comfort for their quaintness and humility and you destroy the picture. It has taken the philistinism of ten Paris municipalities and the callousness of the modern architect to allow in the immediate vicinity of Notre-Dame, round the old "close" where this book is being written, buildings which no stranger can pass without astonishment or derision. But the Middle Ages were foreign to that sentiment: a town consisted of churches, monasteries, scholastic buildings, town hall and ramparts: the rest was of no consequence.

During the sixteenth and seventeenth centuries the same indifference to mere rows of private abodes continued with the picturesque results still before us, but the wealth or ambition of cities appeared in the magnificence of their squares. The Place Royale (now des Vosges) is a revelation of grandeur to many an unsuspecting visitor emerging into it from the surrounding labyrinth. The Palais-Royal Garden and the Place Vendôme offer the same dazzling contrast to their vicinity. Saint Paul's Churchyard in London produces a similar effect, which the parks of modern cities seldom rival.

The mansions bordering those squares could not but be palatial: in fact they remained the models for domestic elegance until almost the present generation. Soon towns broke away from their fortifications, the old ramparts were torn down, making room for magnificent avenues and giving the architect a chance for those garden-surrounded mansions, half town-houses, half château-like *pavillons*, which delighted the eighteenth and the early nineteenth century. From that moment domestic architecture took precedence, with images of elegance and vastness as its background. In fact, the vision of what was to be the modern American city began to replace the medieval picture.

People who have not visited the United States harbor the most fanciful notions about its architecture. The irregularity and commonness of some downtown quarters choked up with telegraph poles deceive the untravelled foreigner who can only judge from pictures. But who can take his first bird's eye view, not only of Chicago or Los Angeles, but of a score more of the larger towns, without admiring the imperial proportions of their plans? Six miles away from the centre of Los Angeles stretch broad avenues planted with magnificent palm-trees which cannot be less than thirty years old. So, thirty years ago, when Los Angeles was still half Spanish and half unknown, some men had the revelation of the fairy-like possibilities of their city and acted accordingly. The most spectacular display of architecture that man can see at the present day, over unbelievably beautiful hills, and under an unrivalled sky is the reward of their wisdom and boldness. I dwell on Los Angeles because it has undoubtedly become the representative American city, but I might quote a long list of other towns. Galveston, of which nobody ever speaks, is built on the same immense scale, and, though supposedly small, is, in reality, a vast and strangely beautiful city. Its charm has the something indefinable and almost preternatural which baffles admiration in the rarest spots on earth.

What is lacking in America, with a few exceptions dating at least a hundred years back, is the beauty of the street as a street. Downtown streets are always ordinary, while everywhere residential quarters have the appearance of parks with houses scattered over them. Even Park Avenue, palatial though it was before sky-scrapers began to break its stately line, shows more juxtaposition than continuity. But when this much has been said, the truth remains that there are in America more beautiful homes than in all the rest of the world together. The American architcct had a tradition to go by. The dry grace of a few old streets in Philadelphia, the pastel elegance of the houses on Boston Hill, the final yet discreet touch on many specimens in Newport, Albany, or Annapolis were models, of course. But while the trend of architecture in most nations has been towards originality, even if it had to be through ugliness, the American architect has had the wisdom to insist primarily on avoiding ugliness. He himself failed during the latter part of the nineteenth century (see the older apartment-houses in Park Avenue) but he has wonderfully succeeded since. People used to make fun of his European-made collections of château-farms, lodges, old stairways, oval windows, timber-gables, turrets, etc., in which he could find either inspiration or motifs inviting imitation; but he loved these forms while their legitimate owners overlooked them, and by dint of loving them he has made them his own. Who can say that there is not an unmistakable American touch on the endless but all too short avenue connecting Chicago with Lake Forest, or on the new Cathedral quarter in Washington? And never, never anything ugly.

Compare what we have to see in France, side by side with the fascinating relics of the past. Look at the cabochon-like new buildings with which modern architects are quickly coarsening the delicate outline of the Paris boulevards; look at the leprosy of hideousness which the local builders have spread in the immediate vicinity of Paris, in what used to be charming Meudon; look at the red belt of brick and tile mercilessly choking the noblest cathedral towns; look at the so-called restoration of the devastated regions! at what has been built round the Cathedral of Rheims! Everything is ugly, ugly!

The marvel is, in spite of that, to hear French architects endlessly talking about the so-called principles on the strength of which they are erecting those deplorable things, and to observe their comical innocence of foreign disappointment, or of the reticence of American Beaux-Arts friends. Because the Perrey brothers succeeded a few times in divorcing modernism from ugliness they think themselves the lineal descendants of Pierre de Corbie. Empty-handed, they go on hoping that something must come of the dreams which they call ideas. They look profound and tortured. One of them, not long ago, said: "You cannot imagine the effort it takes to attain even to ugliness." Impotence, which spoke out in this confession, is the characteristic of those so-called artists, and nothing can redeem them until they acknowledge the fundamental powerlessness to which their vision of an impossible originality has condemned their efforts.

Here and there in Paris we see a faint gleam of hope. Two or three houses in the Place Dauphine have been rebuilt stone for stone. Two buildings between the Pont-Neuf and the old streets leading to Saint-Germain-des-Prés are traditional without being servile. But how short the list is!

While hardly anybody in Europe suspects that America offers the best examples of modern domestic architecture, there is an almost universal conviction that, whether for repute or for disrepute, the sky-scraper is the one American originality. People ask strange questions about it until they are made to understand that a sky-scraper is not a house but a tower.

The tower is a noble thing. Take away their towers from Rouen, Cologne or Antwerp, and the physiognomy of these towns will be hopelessly spoiled. It was written on the site of New York that towers must spring up there. The pity is that there are too many of them. Moreover, they all suffer from the haunting presence of the American ghost, novelty. The ideas of antiquity and permanence are attached to towers, and we cannot shake them away. But an American tower has seldom been forty years where it is standing, and if it has, it is referred to as an "old building" with the secret humiliation which, in America, is the forerunner of destruction. It is difficult to lose one's heart to a structure which has no more duration in it than a World's Fair monument.

It is no less true that the sky-scraper is a great and noble conception. It used to be selfish and would kill whatever was in its vicinity: Trinity Church, in New York, and its graveyard are pathetic witnesses to the fact. But there are clusters of them which somehow arise with the harmony often noticeable in a conclave of Alpine peaks: when the sunset flushes their tops the effect is strangely similar. It cannot be doubted either that the Empire State Building must have been predestined to stand where it is. Look at it from the East River, from any of the Bridges, or from Central Park, it appears to be a final and unescapable thought without which there could have been neither completeness nor proportion. Its presence is so visibly god-willed that we never give a thought to its recency.

In a few cases, the architect has evidently thought tenderly of the humbler buildings as he designed his forty-stories structure. Walk back twenty steps from Park Avenue up East Fiftieth Street, then turn round and look at St. Bartholomew's. It is a beautifully harmonious church on which the light loves to play. The architect who was commissioned to erect the tower at its back felt he could not disregard its appeal. The slender tower was designed as if it actually belonged to the church, and somehow it also lends its elegance to the Cathedral School buildings in the background. The ensemble has picturesqueness as well as unity and its fancifulness does not detract from its style. Many a time I have watched the tower inviting the dome to soar up to its height, and wondered why I was alone in doing so.

But architecture need not always be studied and admired consciously. Swiss mountaineers, with the exception of professional guides whom I have sometimes seen attentive and wistful, seldom look at even their most famous peaks. The people of Carcassonne or Aigues-Mortes mostly seem indifferent. Gradually there is being developed in the New Yorker's consciousness an idea of beauty which, for a time, may be alloyed with local pride but which cannot but result in a moral combination from which dignity will not be absent. Architecture, of all the arts, is the one which acts the most slowly, but the most surely, on the soul.

CHAPTER XIII

Sculpture

SCULPTURE is even more intimidating than architecture of which it was long an adjunct. Few people have a chance to give proper attention to the Parthenon frieze, or the South porch of Chartres cathedral, and they are so dazed, when they study pictures of them, by the multitude of details that they give up in discouragement. Or sculpture is gigantic and frightens women. Hardly anybody can dream of buying statuary, or housing it: too expensive and too bulky. Its proper place, when it happens to come our way, is in the garden. Too often it is in the cemetery. Marble feels cold, bronze without a patine produces annoying reflections, iron is coarse, terra-cotta is cheap, and it takes years to enjoy sculpture in its first garb, clay, still bearing the imprint of the artist's fingers. Official sculpture with which our towns are inundated is ludicrous, modern religious sculpture is disappointing or worse.

When we try to make a systematic study of the sculptor's art we are promptly thrown back on the Ancients, and confronted with the necessity of classical knowledge. If we acquire it, we discover that sculpture has been meditated about, refined and codified to an extent we had no suspicion of, that canons defining the proportions of the body or of the face have been arrived at after centuries of research, and that a book written on the chin in ancient sculpture was not superfluous. Behind these technicalities we feel the presence of a tantalizing wealth of such noble enjoyment that it is equally heart-breaking to go on with an inexhaustible study or to interrupt it.

For, anybody who is interested in sculpture is not slow in recognizing that it is the art of the noble or heroically-minded, the passion of the severely artistic, and that the people who prefer it are the same who prefer poetry to prose. Sculpture magnifies all it touches, whether its characteristic be grace or power. Nobody can approach the major works of Michelangelo without being conscious of this aggrandizing power. But take even a small statue like the *Mercury* of Jean Boullogne—wrongly called of Boulogne for he was born at Douai—visibly intended to convey an impression of grace and lightness: if you look at it long enough to allow the inspiration, the background, and the habitual thoughts of the artist to seep into your own mind, you will soon be conscious of something in that statue superior even to the airiness which at first delighted you. Force is there, the force of the very strong which does not like to show itself: every fibre in that lovely body is in action or ready for action. This is not all: sooner or later, if you persevere in your examination, it will be brought home to you that this *Mercury* is only—like the *Diana,* a few steps away, in the Louvre—part of a general effort of the artist to read ideal beauty into apparently real forms. For that is sculpture's particular vocation.

Are you thinking, in contradiction, of the display in most gothic buildings, of what people generally call realistic sculpture: grimacing devils, tortured dead, or medieval buffoons? Even that kind of sculpture is not realistic, except in the distorted sense lately given to the word: it is interpretative. There is no realistic sculpture, except perhaps on the squares of our towns where bronze politicians in bronze coats pay the penalty for capturing notoriety without having had distinction. That kind of sculpture is to genuine art what photography is to painting and ought to be called by another name. Daniel Chester French's *Lincoln,* in the Washington memorial is also, no doubt, a marble politician in a marble coat. But that statue *is* sculpture, because it is a great idea materialized. Stand at the entrance of the monument for five minutes, and tell me if you can think your every-day thoughts in such a place. That is the test of sculpture as well as its object.

But how should we approach works of sculpture in order to be fashioned by them, according to the spirit of the artist?

You know that mere imitation cannot be called art, and therefore you must not attach any artistic importance to even remarkable feats of manual dexterity. You also know that sentimentality is the natural enemy of sculpture. So, never admire it, always carefully distinguish between sentimentality and sentiment.

Sentiment fills the thoughtful head which Rodin has called *La Pensée,* so exquisitely thought-like and pansy-like that we know its eyes must be violet and we read in them as if they were alive. Next to it comes grace which is multitudinous. It can have a roguish touch as in Carpeaux' *Flore,* or in his Italian boys, or it can be so purely itself that we hesitate in not calling it beauty. When you feel that uncertainty you are ready for the Greeks, and Scopas or even Praxiteles are your sculptors.

From them it is only a step to the finality of the previous period, the supreme epoch which bears the name of Phidias. If what purports to be the work of this prince of sculptors seems to you superhuman to the point of soullessness, remember that, without him, there would have been no Parthenon, and the Parthenon frieze and the British Museum statues detached from the same temple, delight quite as much as they awe. Those sublime works will teach you what esthetics calls style, that is to say, the predominance of the universal even in life-like pieces.

Few among modern artists have had style to the degree in which Bourdelle exhibits it. He is not true to life, you say, his *Heracles* is not a real man. Right, but he is a real god. Those elongated limbs which you criticize, those impossible eyes following an invisible arrow, are the expression of Hercules' divinity. You might as well reproach the sculptor of the Venus of Milo with giving his goddess godlike proportions while refusing her the loveliness of face and figure he could have copied from a hundred models in the island.

But if you once appreciate one great classical piece it will teach you to appreciate all the others, and not only in sculpture but in the other arts as well. Artistic education without sculpture is an impossibility. With it, it becomes a matter of course.

CHAPTER XIV

Painting

Contary to sculpture, painting is the favorite art with modern people: its brilliance, its wizardry, its comparative cheapness, its convenience, the facility with which it can be adapted to household purposes, the sentiment often attached to it, all combine to make it lovable. Most people when they utter the word art see a picture in their mind's eye.

Yet, painting has succeeded in not cheapening itself. The greatest artistic successes, since the sixteenth century, have gone to painters: Raphael, Rembrandt, Rubens, not to recall the extraordinary fortunes of many nineteenth century artists. The best pieces of sculpture never fetch now-a-days the prices unhesitatingly paid for pictures: only jewelry or rare books can rival these on the market. And there are no signs of a change. Dealers have learned the knack of artificially making the productions, even of a prolific painter, scarce. Critics, sometimes unconsciously, are influenced by this commercialization, and we see posthumous notoriety going up and down with values. Add the briskness produced by school controversies. Indeed painting is queen, and nobody is surprised to see her taking precedence in most collections and at all exhibitions.

Popularity should not always be discounted

against merit. Painting undoubtedly is the magical art, unrivalled for illusion. Watch a sculptor at his work: the slowness and difficulty of its progress may easily damp you. Watch a painter: in less than an hour you will see marvellous things happening on his canvas: a church will open for you its marble depths flushed by gorgeous windows; a sunset will glow behind a dark-limbed oak-tree, and even while you see it being painted, you will marvel that it can be painted at all; or you will find that even the air, its quality and transparency, can be suggested by relays of pigment with nothing aerial in them; if a Matisse holds the brush, light, light itself, will emanate from the surface on which the painter plays.

All this is done by processes so similar to conjuring that they puzzle you even when you can watch every detail of them. Take in your hand a small oblong picture by Monet: you can examine it, even with the magnifying glass, for an hour, without being able to guess the subject of it: the two upper thirds of the canvas offer dirty brown surfaces intersected with red splotches: lower down darkish spots unpleasantly suggest flies "swatted" on the none too clean vacant spot. Hang the picture again where you found it and fall back a few steps; how could you have hesitated? This is a festive day with a happy breeze in a blue sky, red bunting furls and unfurls itself in the wind, while in the street, down below, a crowd marches shouting and laughing. Some of the hieroglyphic flies have turned into expressive faces, and there can be no doubt that the crowd is in motion. Marvellous man! He could only be beaten by himself, when half blind but sure of his memory, and sure of his hand, he would torture strange crooked things in red, white or purple, which at the proper distance became happy water-lilies floating on unbelievably transparent water.

The cunning of the painter's hand should never be spoken of except with reverence: it is a rare gift; but the great painter possesses another faculty which is no less wonderful, viz., invention or imagination. On the few occasions when comparatively complete exhibitions of the works of Rembrandt, Turner or Delacroix have been given, it became apparent even to people who knew nothing about their lives that the mental activity of these men was their most admirable trait. Such minds are teeming with images. But the portfolios of many less supreme artists have often been a revelation: the painter is so generally self-contained only because he carries a world in himself.

How should we look at pictures in order to collaborate with the artist instead of misjudging him?

Nobody should ever condemn a painter's method; he may wish us, as the early Flemings did, to scan his work as closely as if it were a jewel, or, on the contrary, he may, like Rembrandt, remind us that oily paint is not sweet-smelling and should be given a wide berth. We should not find fault with his vision either, or declare it inaccurate. We do not possess his trained eye-sight, what Cicero called his "erudite vision"; our own eyes are taught by shabby necessities not to be exacting, they are made to see what they are supposed to see, or what an adjective compels them to see, much more than what they actually mirror. We may not know it, but we actually see blue in snow or bright yellow in vividly lighted grass. When the painter transfers such actualities to his canvas he is right, and, if we blame him, we are simply losing a chance of learning.

We should not attach too much importance to the story told by a picture, and we should be decidedly on our guard against sentimental anecdotes, even dignified by eighteenth century costumes. Millet's *Angelus,* saved in the original by the artist's craftsmanship and by the virginity always attached to originals, has, on account of its subject, become a chromo the reproductions of which are insufferable. There is in the Glasgow Art Gallery a picture by Bastien Lepage, entitled *The Warbler,* representing a little village-girl delightfully coy and bird-like hiding behind a prickly bush. The thing is full of poetry because Bastien Lepage was a poet, but how perilously near the chromo it is! Most popular successes have been due to sentimental touches relieved by prettiness or quaintness. They offend a cultivated eye.

However it is pure snobbery to maintain that subjects are of no importance, and implicitly admit that the Cubist is right in avoiding the very appearance of a subject. Psychology is part of art and so, in spite of long neglect, is composition. Rembrandt never paints without a subject. Would a La Tour portrait lose anything if it were brought into a Watteau scene? We can, to a certain extent, form a correct notion of a painter's temperament by his preference for certain colors or by his touch—Rubens is the classical instance—but the depth of his feeling can only be inferred from his treatment of his subjects. We certainly should not know Rembrandt as we know him had he not etched the Crucifixion. On the other hand, people who are such absolute slaves to *métier* as not to find an exaggeration of sensuousness in Rubens are too timid to be called cultivated.

There is nothing, of course, against which modern people are so set as against prettiness in art. They are right. Bouguereau and Cabanel are saccharine, and even the loveliness of Greuze has long palled upon us. American magazines certainly insult their readers by indefatigably plying them with prettiness or sweetness. But the substitution, for these superannuated attractions, of ugliness or strangeness as the background of refined artistry is another and a worse kind of snobbery. Rodin indeed made his début with *The Man with a broken nose,* and, at the time, this choice was not only daring, it was far-reaching. But Rodin was too great an artist to shut himself up within a category: a brief visit to the Museum in the rue de Varenne will leave no doubt that he delighted in sheer loveliness: to tell the truth, every now and then this appreciation becomes so exaggerated as to seem unhealthy: an orgy of melting curves soon surfeits.

There used to be a time when the final praise of a picture was the exclamation: how life-like! how real! Certainly fidelity to nature will always be one of the guiding principles of art. But what kind of fidelity to nature? It is difficult to open the magazines without encountering the sneezing picture of the boy with a cold in his head, so perfectly life-like that we hastily turn the page over in self-protection.

Yet, is that art? If it is, all the shaving or smoking advertisements are also art, though even a child knows they are not. On the contrary, the action of a badly-drawn horse may be art and it is great art in Seurat's *Circus*. As a matter of fact, art should be truer than life, for we carry in our minds a psychology of human nature which we unconsciously draw upon when we look at an average face and which heightens its relief. A portrait without that relief may be reality itself, it will seem flat.

I had a rare occasion once to find out for myself how indisputable this statement is. I was riding down the rue du Bac on the roof of one of the old horse-busses. As we approached the Seine I was surprised to see an oval portrait of a woman hanging among a score of other gilt frames in the familiar window of a framer there. I had never known that tradesman to sell any pictures and I gave some attention to the portrait. It was an indifferent piece of work, flat, lifeless, and I thought it poorly painted till, to my surprise, it slowly took itself out of the frame and went back to the chair it had probably just left. The so-called portrait was the framer's wife herself, and life trying to masquerade as art had been found wanting.

Finally, we shall do well every time we enter an art collection to remember that the history of painting may mean the history of schools and tendencies, but it also means something strikingly similar to the progress of the boy who teaches himself painting. The stages of his improvement, as well as the varying bourns of his ambition are, first of all, to eliminate from his figures the rough contour which he does not see in nature; then to give them relief: after that he will concentrate on shadows, then on half-shades and on the degradations of light and shade by day or by night, till, finally, he will aspire to the apparently impossible feat of painting light itself. That story of a boy's rising desires also sums up the story of painting in all ages, but more particularly in its latest period. Forget the passionate longing of modern painters to produce pure light effects and you will be unjust to all artists who have come since Turner or Delacroix.

If you remember this simple advice, if you prefer to art critics who insist on speaking in jargon the more nutritious information which a man like Reynolds can give you in plain honest English, if you visit modern galleries without prejudice or famous museums without superstition, you will learn a great deal, which is something, and you will enjoy even more, which is what really matters. But it is all-important that we should not fumble our way through more or less celebrated galleries. We ought never to approach one without being as clear about its history, arrangement and object as about the past and present of any town we are planning to visit.

Museums vary greatly in object. The Vatican is merely a princely collection of masterpieces. The Brera at Milan aims at no universality, but is invaluable for the story of the Northern schools; the National Gallery in London is probably the most satisfactory collection in the world, for it excludes all mediocrity and yet manages to present in orderly succession the chronology of the schools; the American museums frequently consist of separate donors' collections which have to be examined as if they were distinct galleries; the Chicago Art Institute which twenty-five years ago showed an ideal presentment of the history of art, even American art, is now over-crowded and clamors for re-arrangement; the Louvre, which is the richest collection in the world, is positively a problem and, too often, it is also a puzzle.

It is, of course, a magnificent structure, but it is not always good for an art collection to be housed so palatially. The royal proprietors of the Louvre did not build the palace for the collection, they bought the collection for the palace. That it was so is still visible from the catalogue, full of references to past arrangements to which the visitor is indifferent, and it is no less visible in the presentment of the works of art themselves. Neither the *Venus of Milo* nor the *Victory* are where they should be to guide the student, they are where they have inevitably to be the moment they are in the Louvre. Again, the collection is too large and it is of unequal value because, for a hundred and fifty years, the Long Gallery was used for the Salons and many of the exhibits of yore were left there. If you do not know those historical details you run the risk of misjudging the Museum or of being dazed by it. Similar remarks might be made about most other famous collections.

The authorities who look after public galleries too often forget that those collections are not meant for their own private enjoyment, but are democratic institutions intended to facilitate the artistic education of a nation. That carelessness is unforgivable, but it is practically universal, and visitors had better be prepared to face it.

Discouraging? Everything concerning education is. But with a modicum of method, a few good books and a little oral information which is not difficult to obtain, you can extract from a museum all the education and all the pleasure it is capable of giving. The education, it should never be forgotten, is in direct proportion to the pleasure. That is the unique privilege of art.

CONCLUSION

People often say: the machine and beauty are irreconcilable: one of the two must perish, and as it is obvious that the machine is in the ascendant the chances for an ideal civilization are weak.

Much of such a sweeping statement can be challenged and is contradicted by facts. It is true that the machine is in the ascendant, but why? Undoubtedly because mankind demands an easier life, craves more freedom and leisure. If the machine does not give that, it will be despised and hated as it was in *Erewhon.* But every sign indicates that if man is determined not to let the machine dictate to him, he can make it his slave and leisure will be the result.

But along with leisure modern hedonism wants pleasure. What kind of pleasure? Evidently the humbler and lower satisfactions being the more accessible are generally preferred, and this tendency gives our epoch its appearance of banality. However, it is no less evident that the preferences which are alive in the artist are dormant in the average man and only need to be awakened. Many times in the past mankind has had its choice between materialism and civilization and has not chosen badly: the Greek Republics, Rome, the Italian Republics, London and Paris at their best are well-known examples. And what is the meaning of the stupendous effort which, during the past forty years, America has been making to beautify itself with bricks or trees? No, the machine age is not inevitably an ugly age.

If we say that hedonism can hardly be called a noble doctrine the answer will be that there are pleasures and pleasures. The moment admiration comes into play, not only does the level of pleasure rise at once, but it becomes tinged with ethical distinction. We cannot admire beauty and callously bear with our own personal ugliness. Plato rightly says, in his *Republic:*

"Even the less gifted men, if they happen to grow up among the masterpieces of architecture, sculpture and painting, will imbibe a taste for beauty and decency: they will learn to find out what is perfect or what is deficient in nature and art, and this rectitude of judgment will gradually spread over to their souls."

Beauty in art is indeed the natural introduction to beauty in life.

PART THREE

BONUM

OR BEAUTY IN LIFE

INTRODUCTORY NOTE

Part One of this book is an attempt at showing the kind of thought-material likeliest to give full play to our intellect in a field high above the ordinary. Part Two, which we have just concluded, also strives to raise us above our daily routine by the enjoyment of natural, artistic, or literary beauty. This Part Three will deal with the third element capable of giving nobility to a human existence. Philosophers call it Goodness, but we shall soon see that, in reality, it is another form of beauty. Only, whereas esthetics—at all events the production of beauty—and also metaphysics, require a special gift and some training as well as favorable circumstances, we all have about equal chances to make our life beautiful. I have seen rare dignity in many a peasant, and simple lives can be great. Life is given to all of us to make what we please of it: a masterpiece or a shabby piece of work. We are born with an infallible instinct to recognize what will satisfy our higher tendencies, what will give us at the same time the influence to which every man has a right and the happiness which we all crave. No gift here is necessary and no exceptional chances. All we need is our desire and a method. Consciously or unconsciously, the desire is so deeply rooted in us that even a whole life-span of vulgarity does not succeed in killing it. As for the method, it is simplicity itself, and has been discovered by hundreds of soul-gardeners independent of one another.

A few chapters will be added showing that the search after moral beauty is either a form of religion or inevitably leads to contact with spiritual realities.

A. THE PLANE OF MORAL BEAUTY

CHAPTER I

Moral Beauty

As EACH one of us consists of matter and spirit, so is mankind composed of Materialists and Idealists. It is useless to add that materialists win, at least in so far as plurality counts.

The materialism of worldlings is not avowed, of course, nor is it blatant or defiant, but it feels in possession, it is calm and unruffled. Millions and millions seem perfectly satisfied with their petty but cosy downstairs. What do they do there? Their characteristic is that, in a classical phrase of moralists, the meaning of which has been completely transformed since the days of Jean-Jacques Rousseau, "they always follow nature", that is to say, go down the primrose path, or only do what can be done with the minimum effort. Indolent, of course, lazy and spineless. But as feebleness hates whatever makes it realize its precariousness, they are also fearful of all disturbances, and selfish.

Not selfish enough or unwise enough, however, to be unkind when it is not necessary. Seldom cruel. Selfishness knows that remorse and shame are annoying, and that crumpled up rose-leaves offend the connoisseur in comfort. So a commonwealth of intelligent egoism has been built by the millions, and a skilful combination of the idealism of the few with the contributions of the many has largely eliminated from it all that might cause irritation or shame. Many people seem to live and die without noticing that they have never done anything for anybody but themselves.

This, however, except in the case of exceptional good fortune, or exceptional stupidity, is only an appearance. A certain smile of young people, willing to be egotists but fearing the danger of looking like fools, or a certain shrug of veteran worldlings, especially women, are the masonic signs of the brotherhood of self-love. What do these signs mean? As plainly as words they mean: I am a fraud; I live a lie; I manage to secure occupation without producing action; I have learned how to get rid of vacuum without delivering substance; I call other people jesuitical—the most slanderous of adjectives—but I am a past master of compromise; I should hate to be exposed.

Such thoughts are uncomfortable and have to be exorcised. This is done by resorting to heavily sugared pills: lip-service, superficial agitation for a good cause, dancing for the distressed and so forth. The notion that by dressing with real elegance, adorning one's self with perfect taste, keeping a house beautiful or satisfying critical guests, one provides work for people who need it salves one's conscience. But flashes of sincerity will show the unreality of all this. We entertain no doubt, at bottom, that there is something disgraceful in having to be propped up by such flimsy supports. Every now and then we discover in the seething mass of humanity round us a person who does not seem to need anybody else, and the contrast with ourselves is stinging. It is then that we remember some little talent we have not been energetic enough to cultivate and make a slight effort to revive it. Sportive people are conscious of good air, well-being and all that, but they are not unconscious of the mysterious fact that a good tennis-player who otherwise might be a boor is, thanks to his talent alone, half-way towards being a gentleman.

No matter how effective such substitutes for real distinction may be, they never can be effective with everybody all the time. A chance revelation is enough to expose their falsity. Aristotle, with his infallible directness, defines Barbarians as people "insisting on doing what they please, without submitting to any rule." Let such a sentence fall on our peace and it will be replaced at once by restlessness, with touching but feeble attempts at a little serious reading, a better kind of conversation, or a few pilgrimages to an out-of-the-way church where the preacher is reported actually to wake up his hearers.

This means that, in spite of our camouflage, in spite of the vast camouflage of so-called civilization or of the "world", we cannot help realizing, at times, the difference between vegetating and real living. In spite of millions of acts apparently indicating that we prefer nothing to something, our scale of values can never be obnubilated and is only abjured by grossness at its coarsest or by cynicism at its most brazen. We never make a mistake in grading our own actions or in discriminating between the serious or the frivolous periods of our life. We look back with wonder and regret at the days when we were young and generous. There have been minutes in our existence when almost unexpectedly, we have done something which might almost be called heroic. The recollection of those moments is satisfactory, but there is something imperious in it which is not entirely comfortable, for we now feel unequal to what formerly seemed so easy. No matter how cob-webbed our moral lantern, its little light is still steady.

If we seldom make a mistake in grading our own actions we never make any in estimating other people's, no matter how seductive their appearances may be. Heroism of course we always bow to. I have never forgotten a scene at the Nevers hospital during the war. A convoy of wounded soldiers had arrived in the night and most of them were ready, the next morning, for the surgeon's inspection. A man of about forty, with a stern expression, lay with his whole chest exposed. Just above his heart, so near the heart that the thought of the narrow escape made one shiver, blushed a neat wound. The bullet had passed clean through the body, but no vital organ had been hurt and the soldier could speak in his natural voice.

In August 1914 he was employed in the Argentine, on an *estancia* at a riding distance of eighteen days from the coast. One morning he was on horseback, going west, and singing a French song, when he met a few *gauchos,* riding in the opposite direction. One of these men, hearing the French song, turned his horse's head towards him. "You're French," he said, "so am I. War has been declared. I am going to Buenos Aires to see the consul and sail as soon as I possibly can."

"War declared against us!" replied the other man, "I am going too." And here he was. An eighth of an inch lower the bullet would have silenced his baritone voice and dimmed his bold straight-looking eyes. There was deep silence in the ward as this Ivan Narok told his tale; yet, most of the soldiers there could have matched it in twenty different ways.

However, heroism in capital letters is not necessary for us to exercise our sense of nobility, and neither fame nor talent, nor grace are enough to prevent us from exercising it. There are painful details in the life of Napoleon. Pass from one of Alfred de Musset's *Nights* to some of his love-letters: the contrast will almost give you physical pain. I remember once whiling away a few moments with one of the popular New York magazines. There was on the cover the inevitable picture of a cinema star with no soul at all in her starry eyes, and there were pictures of an internationally famous sculptor, and of Signor Mussolini at his most searching and most invading. Finally there was one of a Jewish philanthropist whose name was entirely unfamiliar. This was a youngish man whose face told you his whole story at a glance: the man had suffered and he could not bear either to see other people suffering, or to find himself unable to help them in their fight. I cut out that picture and I have preserved it: its wistfulness preaches to me more eloquently than many a famous treatise. Why did I prefer it to that of the powerful statesman or to that of the wizard artist? Because everybody would have made the same choice. Because the attraction, that is to say, the beauty was of a higher order. William James says in his unique way: "A deep and ineradicable instinct exists in each one of us preventing him from regarding life as a mere joke or at best as an elegant comedy. No! life is an austere tragedy and what we relish the most in it is the bitterest it has to offer. On the scene of the world heroism, heroism alone, plays the great parts. In heroism, we realize it, lies hidden the mystery of life. A man is nothing if he is incapable of sacrifices. On the other hand, evident though the shortcomings of a man may be, if he is ready to give up his life for a cause, we forgive him everything. However inferior he may be to ourselves in other respects, if we cling to life while he throws it away like a flower, we bow to his superiority."

Even the most debased individual, in his heart of hearts, knows that this is true.

Vaguely or definitely we also agree about something else. We somehow connect this persistence of a right moral judgment, in spite of a low existence, with the presence of the Spirit in the world. We have no doubt that moral Beauty is only an aspect of Truth which is synonymous with God. We know that the amount of it in the world is in proportion to the amount of freedom allowed by us to the spiritual element in our souls. Hence that consciousness of a divine command which we have grown accustomed to call Duty.

But we dislike the words Duty, divine command, or divine ordinances, quite as much as the words moral or righteous. Not that we are afraid of sounding pious or preachy if we use these words, but we do not like the feeling that we must be good because we are told to be so. We hate orders and obedience; we promptly accuse people who use these words of clinging to a superannuated anthropomorphic idea of the Deity. We want our morals to be based on choice and freedom, not on submission to an enforced scale of values.

This attitude is not of yesterday. What, towards the end of the nineteenth century, was called the crisis of morals was nothing else. People wanted to do good because they preferred it, not because they were expected to do it. As in most rebellions there was a basis for their attitude. We do not want our natural impulses to be dictated to; we feel as if acting right upon orders was not acting right as we should. We believe in attraction and not in compulsion.

The Greeks, more than twenty centuries back, must have felt something of the same uncertainty. Boys at school wonder why the two words *kalon,* the beautiful, and *agathon,* the right, should have been fused by the Greek language into one word, *kalonkagathon,* applying to the whole range of morals. It is no doubt because they were so overwhelmingly conscious of the beauty of morally superior lives that the Greeks had to compel their language to express this conviction. In the same way, though with far less profundity, medieval French denoted goodness and bravery by one word. It is one of the miracles of Satan, or of thoughtlessness, that what is good should ever have ceased to be regarded as beautiful, and that our most natural instinct should have been made to feel ill-treated when it is indulged. Moral beauty is pre-eminently attraction. Here is a case not of jumping into a corral or struggling into a straitjacket, but of making the most of one's best, of finding one's self and one's climate, of making sure of happiness through self-fulfilment.

CHAPTER II

Possibility of Attaining to Moral Beauty

We believe in it. Our imagination constantly shows us the acquisition of moral superiority as possible. All children imagine they are Robinson Crusoes, but who has ever been able to read Silvio Pellico's *Mie Prigioni,* or Dostoevsky's *The House of the Dead* without a haunting desire of going, or at all events, of having gone, through the same experiences? The prison background may be horrible, but the reflection of the grandeur developing in spite of it lends poetry to the suffocating Venetian jail or to the dreary Siberian camp. We constantly catch ourselves imagining that we can copy what we admire, even the talent of an artist, even physical excellence. It is a well-known law of esthetics that the more perfect a work of art is, the simpler we believe its execution must have been.

What strikes us at once in superior lives is their magnetism: moral beauty has only to show itself immediately to gather a following. The longing to possess the same magic is never resisted. We want influence and we want it of the right kind. The reproach that we drag other people down or merely that our attitude causes surprise, bad enough when our conscience whispers it, is unbearable when we have to hear it expressed in clear words by somebody we respect. How worthless then seem the petty satisfactions we have been foolish enough to prefer to real joys! And how natural the choice from which we have recoiled becomes to our retrospective view! For there is a beginning of possession every time we are conscious of urgent attraction, even if it is that of the inaccessible Alpine glacier. Indeed our whole life is one continuous, if often unconscious, certainty that the beautiful images we cannot help gathering on the way must, in the near future, become realities and transform our humdrum existence.

But do people ever get transformed by their nobler desires? Is not the haunting certainty just mentioned a mere delusion which a hundred disappointments somehow never dispel? What does our experience show us if not people growing more sceptical and weaker as they grow wiser?

It is true that what we see is not encouraging, but it is also true that we sometimes fail to see what would be encouraging. The revolutionists who once plotted with Pellico against Austria, or with Dostoevsky against Czarism, had no idea in their prisons of what was going on in their former companions' souls. We do not like the word conversion which seems to connote a surrender and has become rather technical, but transformations happen every day in people who, till then, showed no symptoms of being transformed. Let alone the case of Saint Paul which stands apart, but what about Augustine or Ignatius of Loyola? Was not the former a typical intellectual without much force, and was not the latter an average hidalgo soldier, undistinguishable from scores of others serving in the King of Spain's armies? Yet, the day came when both men were dissatisfied with their existence and started on an entirely different one. Are there not phases, a visible ascent, in the early part of Emerson's career?

Great men? Famous and exceptional instances, so often alluded to that some unreality has finally attached to them and they are not quite so persuasive as they used to be? But shall we say that the language which speaks of turning a new leaf, of rising to an occasion, or of rising above one's self, is also unreal? The same progress visible in an artist's, or perhaps in a business man's, career can take place, and does take place, in people's moral development. One day a disgust of the selfish average comes upon them and they are never the same after that revelation: or a chance offers itself to do a big thing not exactly appealing, and they do not recoil from it and henceforth they are saints without knowing it.

But on innumerable occasions there is no visible change in people's lives. They gain their perfection as we accumulate wisdom, imperceptibly. I remember a château in which the servants who glided around were as silent as monks and as polite as dukes. Nobody, not even themselves, could have said how they had acquired that manner. There are infinitely fewer Christians than the statistics say, but there are far more than the world suspects or likes to imagine. The first quality of those daily-improving lives is that they do not let anybody see their steady development. But what need have we to look round for what we can find in ourselves? There is probably not a single man or woman who, mostly from self-interest, it is true, but it might also have been from a superior motive, has not overcome powerful obstacles and accomplished things extremely difficult to undertake. Does not Charles Kingsley rightly say that "in the pettiest character there are unfathomable depths"?

There are many obstacles, no doubt, in the way of our moral improvement, but when they can be approached and estimated they appear to be more numerous than formidable, mirages most of them. The most obvious kind is supposed to be a lack of favorable circumstances. We know that Lincoln, ready though he was, only grew to his full stature after the war gave him his chance. We also know how much anonymous heroism was elicited by the Great War which otherwise would have remained dormant. But who can wish for such a chance? The thought might be enough to make us relapse into our usual nervelessness. Wrongly, for Lincoln may have needed a war to attain to his full stature, but his biography, or some other great man's biography, or some one of the books of wisdom likely to come within the reach of most of us, have many times been sufficient to give our torpor the necessary awakening.

Some people, it is true, are afraid of heroism as they are afraid of great literature, of poetry, or of anything that sounds apart and above. "Would you like to be a saint?" I once asked a girl of great natural refinement, but more subtle than forceful. *"Yes,"* was the answer, *"only my parents would not like it."* The girl did not know that if she had been a saint her parents, as is invariably the case, would have been spell-bound by her saintliness. More probably her imagination showed her aloofness from her father and mother as a condition of holiness, which of course it was not. I have seen many people in love with the little saint of Lisieux, Sister Thérèse, as long as they could think of her as a pretty young nun, of rare spiritual attraction, no doubt, but brought nearer to us by the charming things she said about roses. Quote in their hearing some one of the austere-sounding speeches which are natural to saints, and which abound in Sister Thérèse's life, they would instantly shrink away from her. Yet heroism is only magnetic because it is simple and, at bottom, natural.

The worst obstacles to a higher life are indolence which is cowardly, and gregariousness which gives us the semblance of a reason for not rising above the average. Indolence never begins anything. If it did begin something it would not persevere. Many people are persuaded that a book is an idea. It has to be that, no doubt, but it is quite as much an achievement of will-power. A book, like anything requiring protracted attention, is a fight with laziness. So is the correction of one fault. So is the renunciation of the fascination of trifles.

Gregariousness is the multiplication of indolence by millions. It is useless to recall the rather sickening slogans to which it gives currency in the world. What we call civilization is not altogether good for us: it makes things too easy. Imagine the ingenuity and the energy which primitive man had to display to get his dinner. Imagine the experiments and the divination necessary for him to be sure about the qualities of plants. His mind must have been alert all the time. Sluggishness, visible in innumerable living examples, is the most formidable deterrent from any high moral initiative. And it is caused not so much by the difficulty of things as by the spectacle of mankind acting as if everything were difficult and yet not only surviving but being rather comfortable.

How can these obstacles, or apparent obstacles, be overcome? As usual by a substitution of motive images for inert ones, by a certain amount of guidance and by the knowledge of a method. A writer who starts work on a subject without knowing anything of its bibliography, must feel he is working blindly. Fumbling and blind must also be the effort towards improvement which a man makes in ignorance of long-discovered but generally forgotten methods. It is to these methods that we must now advert.

CHAPTER III

How We Can Attain to Moral Beauty

First by changing our views and then by modifying our life.

All our actions are regulated by our principles, but our principles are merely summaries from impressions accompanying the most active images or sets of images in our mind. Some people will mostly be conscious of mental images showing to them "good times", others will see good deeds reproduced with equal clarity on their interior screen. Inevitably the former will regard good times as the natural object of their activity, while the latter will think them inferior to the images dominant in their minds.

One image, if it happens to collect round itself exceptional energy, may be enough to force upon us either the triviality of one kind of existence, or the distinction of its contrary, and this may take place in an instant. Hazlitt, telling us the story of his infatuation for a girl as inferior to him as Fanny Brawne was to Keats, gives us an instance of a phenomenon of that kind. The spell fell away from him "as an insufficiently glued post-stamp will come off a letter". The real picture of the lady was substituted for an illusion, that was all. Psychologists tell us that a habit can be formed in a second and may endure a lifetime. All depends on the power of the mental image.

It must be admitted that irresistible images are as scarce as celebrated religious conversions. We constantly see images tending to raise us above our daily existence, but we see them as we may catch a glimpse of a forest glade from a car. In a moment, the fleeting image is replaced by rivals, and only leaves something unidentified, pulling at our heart-strings. Any revelation of a superior life should be treasured as the precious seed of a rare plant and treated as tenderly.

The first step to be taken is to interrupt the rush of our life which leaves everything barren behind it. It can be done. The beginning of this slackening process can be made quite simply. When you have felt hurried all day, and, towards tired five o'clock, find yourself in the streets of a busy American town, with your jaws locked by fatigue and a feeling of something—your remaining energy—pushing you on, as it seems, by the shoulders, walk a little way out of the crowd, and, during a few minutes, slacken your gait as much as your nerves will let you, looking on the ground and allowing yourself to think that you have a right at least to five minutes' slowness. Soon you will feel out of the rush and superior to it. In the same way, when we hear the invitation to a life which will not consist of an endless succession of trifles, we must try to live to the quiet tock of a grandfather's clock and not to the nagging tick-tick of a modern timepiece. If possible seek a quiet nook, or reduce your schedule, during a few days, so that you may have some feeling of repose. Whatever leisure you can thus save devote it, first of all, to an inventory of yourself.

No such inventory can ever be made by a person entirely satisfied with himself, or who, if he admits shortcomings, admits them with the complacent "Well, I am like that" or "The Lord made me what I am", which has some charm, perhaps, when associated with sweet seventeen but otherwise is pretty sickening. It is not so simple as it seems to make an examination of conscience corresponding to a business investigation. Not always because people, being as a rule indulgent to themselves, are inclined to treat their faults tenderly. The reason lies rather in the difficulty to see beyond disconnected details, or, on the contrary, beyond rough blocks in one's consciousness. If you take up a spiritual book and try to feel duly humble and self-contemning, you may not be helped one bit in your effort to see yourself as you really are. You will probably hear vague self-condemnatory sentences in your inner ear, but they will not convince you.

As a matter of fact an investigation of ourselves, with our possibilities and impossibilities, should be conducted according to general intellectual rules. Paper, as usual, will help. If you begin with a collection of memoranda referring to a number of things in which you think your disposition is revealed ("talked till everybody hated me"—"furious at so-and-so for not making more of me") you will be going through the operation in a truly scientific manner. For, in a few months, even weeks, when you classify those cards according to the analogies or occurrences they record, your true picture will appear in the sub-titles which you will be adding to the notes. Again, you can write two pen-portraits of yourself, one supposed to come from a not too indulgent friend, the other from an intelligent and witty enemy. Your real likeness will be obtained by putting the criticisms of the friend beside the half-praises of the enemy.

It will be wise to submit these documents to as trustworthy a psychoanalyst as you can find, to the sincere friend who was supposed to write the portrait just mentioned, or to an adviser who will be surprised by your honest interest in your better self. You will then know what a real confession means, and how much it helps. If you have been absolutely frank you will also know how much it costs to admit, for instance, that one is envious, or so conceited that even the smile of a friendly critic makes one wince.

This first step in our mental transformation is the most unpleasant and, although it may not be the most necessary, is nevertheless indispensable. If we want to know the whole truth about ourselves this examination will have to be renewed till we learn the endless variety of self-love's disguises. But even the most accurate knowledge of our deficiencies would not help our ascent to a higher level if we were not attracted to it by something more encouraging than austere truth.

The vision of our transformed self is the real motive power in our transformation. "Beware of illusions" is an excellent motto, but an honest desire, no matter how closely associated it may be with mere air-castles, is not an illusion: it is the foundation of all human action. We stand a far better chance of becoming useful to our community if we optimistically visualize ourselves rivalling great reformers or philanthropists, than if the drooping image of our inadequacy is constantly before us. Even saints must make plans, or indulge in dreams. Wishes are fathers to deeds as well as to thoughts.

When I was a student I had a spiritual guide—not a psychoanalyst—who somewhat puzzled me by repeating every time I saw him: "What you need are convictions; you must acquire convictions." Somehow the word conviction would awaken intellectual associations in my mind and the convictions I was supposed to lack appeared to me as a dry list of self-evident propositions. One day, the same piece of advice being given me, I blurted out: "I honestly don't know what you mean by *convictions;* all I have are desires."—"Why!" the old gentleman said, "your desires are only the imaginative side of your convictions." That meant, of course, that if our mind imparts permanence to a desire for improvement it becomes a principle. But an image is more vital than a principle. Washington's little hatchet has made more truthful boys than the repetition of the principle: we must tell the truth.

The vision of our transformed self will also be profitably connected with what is now, or used to be in the past, our better self. Just as we can help our memory of a historic period by hinging our facts to a few dates remembered from school days, we can make our imaginary future more nearly possible by building it on our solid past. An old diary, a few letters written by us and returned after the death of a friend, may not only be more encouraging, but more serviceable to us than any amount of advice. There is not a single man who has not had great moments, has not risen to rare occasions. If we replace ourselves in the state of consciousness in which we were at those times, we shall in reality be in the condition in which our best becomes possible to us.

Sometimes help may come from unexpected quarters. A friend of mine used to dislike his Lenten diet: he coaxed himself to like it by persuading himself that he never felt better than during those severe weeks. Am I recommending egoism? Heaven forbid! But what helps helps and, whatever intransigent heroisms may proclaim, every step in the right direction counts.

Needless to add that, as we try to people our imagination with helpful visions, nothing will be found so encouraging as the biographies of great men and women particularly attractive to us. However, even such biographies should be carefully criticized. Four pages read at random will be enough to satisfy you whether the author belongs to the old school of admiration at all costs, or to the new school of contemptuous familiarity. The very rhythm of the narrative will let you know whether you are wading through a funeral oration from which you will have to extract the truth by diligent historical criticism, or whether you are in the not very clean hands of the "debunker". The golden mean is rare. If you hesitate, a few of the original documents on which the biographies were built will promptly tell you the truth. A letter or two, the accurate reports of a speech or two will give you more insight into the character you are interested in than fifty pages of comment. You will find that good men were human, after all, but there have been more good men than is dreamt of in the philosophy of writers who either find it hard to believe in goodness, or who have persuaded themselves that readers relish contempt more than admiration.

Books of wisdom, the great books of all nations, should be read too, of course. We like moral formulas as much as we dislike metaphysical ones. The Bible is an inexhaustible mine of such moral sayings. We may find to-day something *bourgeois*, anti-feminist, and generally *arriéré* in the Biblical Wisdom Books, but a manuscript collection of great speeches collected by oneself from the New Testament will provide reflection for a lifetime. Contemporary literature dealing with the guidance of our thought and conduct cannot be disregarded either by the reader equipped to criticize it. There is no greater mistake than to study eternal questions exclusively in old books or exclusively in modern books. The spirit of many of the so-called up-to-date moralists will often be found to be not only anti-clerical, but anti-christian, and often anti-theistic. In spite of this tone or attitude these books have the merit of presenting questions as they present themselves to most of their readers. Moreover they often strive to be fair. Whoever knows how to listen to an author's voice as he goes on with his book will have no doubt that the effort of many modern writers is rather to salvage than destroy.

Let me point out finally that, as we proceed with our reading and thinking, it will be of immense advantage to us to forget that vast majority of our fellow-men or women who fritter away their lives in childish amusements, to feel at one, on the contrary, with the minority, larger than is often supposed, which is engaged in a quest similar to our own. Thousands and thousands all over our planet are trying at this minute, and precisely like ourselves, to escape from the commonplace. Let us remember that we are members of a powerful community. We hear a great deal now-a-days about "Harmony", about diffusing the best of our influence through a sense of harmony. Miracles of healing are supposed to be wrought in that way. Perhaps. But why will mankind always think of physical cures when it hears the word miracle? Certainly, our moral transformation is more important than physical health, and there is no doubt but it can be helped by communion with the invisible friends striving, like ourselves, to disengage their spirit from matter. It is difficult to resist Lamarck's view that evolutionary progress is the result of a vital effort, vague, if you like, but powerfully active in the mysterious regions where it works.

CHAPTER IV

A New Life

IF, BY wishing, thinking and reading we succeed in changing our outlook on life, it will be hardly possible for us not to change our life as well. Asceticism, which means less self-depriving than keeping away from tyrannical trifles, is natural to us. Whenever we become aware of an incipient transformation which can make us a healthful ferment among our fellow-men, we deliberately keep away from the so-called pleasures which, by bringing us down to the common level, might destroy the possibilities we cherish. The certainty that we have discovered the secret of being freer than we were, and of making our neighbor also freer, places responsibilities upon us. We feel compelled to make definite reforms in our ways of living. As usual, the best way to map out those reforms will be to sit down, foresee, draw our conclusions from what we foresee, and, as we proceed with this examination, write down its results. Almost from the beginning we shall be conscious of the necessity to renounce certain habits and certain companies. Psychoanalysts of all degrees constantly advise keeping away from people, sometimes very near to us, who are supposed to be in the way of our self-realization. Nice little bits of cruelty are not infrequently the result.

Selfishness can never be encouraged by idealism, but self-protection is a necessity. If daily experience shows me that I am never my better self when I am with so-and-so, I shall feel like avoiding so-and-so. If the sheet of paper which helps me to conduct my examination makes it clear that a certain correspondence invariably elicits a tone of which I have no reason to be proud, I shall know that I have to rarefy that correspondence or modify it. Saint Teresa of Avila regarded her confessors with such veneration that she felt sure they must be above possible bruises to their vanity. In consequence she frequently waived their services without a qualm. What hagiologists mean by saying that saints seek their own perfection only refers to the saints' consciousness of the obstacles in their way and to their resolute way of ignoring them. They sometimes walk over them, as Saint Jeanne de Chantal, the canonized grandmother of Madame de Sévigné, literally did. She wanted to enter a convent, her children, who adored her, tried to keep her from doing so by actually lying across the hall, and she walked over them. Many people who will blame her for this determination would no doubt approve if she had been leaving home to marry a second husband as perfect as her late one had been. This shows that we all prefer our own method of reaching perfection, or, in the modern parlance which some people use with such unction, our own method of enriching our personality. We only differ about objects.

There will be other obstacles, not quite so exterior to ourselves, to be anticipated. The dread of appearing as a moral "highbrow" is not the least formidable. A strange perversion shows us distinction, even long before we have secured it, in the light of a reproof, rather than a help, to our neighbor. Many people have also been discouraged from beginning by the prospect of the long time it must take them to achieve completion. They forget that unto each day sufficeth the evil thereof, that I can compile a whole dictionary by writing two pages of it every day, or paint my fresco by concentrating on four square inches of it at a time. The job of perfecting oneself is fascinating enough not to be scamped or squandered. What is important is to make a beginning, with the encouraging certainty that many people, not any more gifted than we are, have succeeded in transmuting their ordinariness into magnetic qualities.

This transformation is effected by creating in oneself new habits of a more refined nature than those they are intended to replace. The French language constantly alludes to mental habits which it calls *plis,* kinks, causing us to say or do things which are not natural to us, even though they have found little resistance in us. It is those habits that we have to replace by others. In most cases the transformation proceeds from outside inside. No saint, however humble or determined to look like a beggar, has ever been called ungentlemanly. Saints do not do things which would offend the refined as a mark of inferior breeding. They are not easy-going, effusive, or hail-fellow-well-met. They do not show a lack of dignity by a lack of regard. They may not always seem thoughtful of others because they are too full of their own thoughts, but they will never be found to be invasive, as society people often are. They charm and delight the artist, the moral observer, the seeker of rare characteristics, all the subtle, in fact, by a sense of nuances which is never displayed but is never found at fault either. Superior Hindoos are well-known instances, but monasteries would provide a thousand types equally fascinating if they were not defended by enclosures and silence.

This outward charm is what attracts at first the novices in quest of self-improvement. The mistake has been made by many of them to be satisfied with appearances. Dandyism is not so artificial as it seems. In a certain degree it ceases to be ridiculous because the outward effort works inwards and a moral transformation is produced, almost unawares, by a person who, at the outset, only looked for effect. I have known a person who was not only sincere but right in affirming that an hour spent in the La Tour room, at the Louvre, did more for him than a sermon. Silent commune with those aristocratic gentlemen, witty abbés, and archly smiling marquises, with the delight taken in them by old Quentin de La Tour still floating in the air, cast an irresistible spell upon him! Many years ago, I met a man whose name sounded aristocratic though it was really not so. This peculiarity had produced in its possessor a desire which something accidentally racial in his face had encouraged. The man was visibly trying to look, speak and act like a duke. The effort could not be said to be futile, but it was, like that of a clever actor, accompanied by a satisfaction at its comparative success which was self-accusatory. Not long ago I met the same person still straight and alert, but a septuagenarian. The sense of effort was gone, the old appearances were still preserved, and as the wisdom and mellowness of years had associated their sincerity with what formerly was only pretence, there stood an extremely impressive old man. As aristocratic qualities find it difficult to survive in modern environment, it occurred to me that here was an excellent model for titled young officers or diplomats to copy. Yet its attractiveness was acquired and not inherited.

Many people have made, or will make, a similar effort to beautify themselves in order to be admired. They are not hypocrites, they are not even exactly selfish, they are connoisseurs in charm and they are vain. Look at the published, or publicity, photographs of many writers or artists. One glance is enough to tell us that they have been impressed by the expression of some soulful person, a monk perhaps, and are trying to copy it. When Maeterlinck, before he was forty, wrote his wisdom books, he was obviously more attracted by the outward dignity of saintliness than by its deeper magnetism. An effect was intended much more than renouncement was desired. To use the great modern word, shamelessly displayed in the titles of scores of books, success is what counts with many people trying to appear what they are not, or to secure influence without even the minimum effort.

But only men and women less finely gifted than M. Maeterlinck can be satisfied with a mere semblance. All honest striving after perfection will regard this so-called success as a failure, and the respect it may win will seem to be nothing else than a punishment. Hence the inevitability, for anyone who feels himself called to a higher life, to want more than the qualities which make a socially distinguished person, more than those, no matter how necessary, which go into the make-up of a real gentleman or a real lady. Whitman says it well: "All changes of appearances without a change in that which underlies appearances, are without avail." But is a deeper transformation possible than that which secures admiration for us?

Montaigne, apparently, did not think so when he wrote more cryptically than he generally does: "I cannot find myself where I look for myself." Some moralists even go further. President Wilson said: "There is no more priggish business in the world than the development of one's character." Clearly people who are inclined to take that view are convinced that we can only make those changes of appearances which Whitman regards as useless. Therefore the trouble is not worth taking. I myself used to think that the acquisition of qualities we do not possess by birthright is as chimerical as the acquisition of genius or of charm. I used to watch with some amusement the efforts which a college friend of mine was making to replace his natural stiffness by kindlier ways. When he strove to appear at his most debonair a freezing conviction would come over me that he was torturing himself. Then I would remember that the author of the *Imitation* may say: "We should soon be perfect if we would only conquer one fault every year", but he never speaks of annexing qualities. However, since those far-away years, not only have I seen people poorly gifted intellectually succeed in strengthening their faculties tenfold by diligence and method, but I have actually seen that very schoolfellow of mine achieve his object: nobody can approach him now without being conscious of kindliness in which one thoroughly believes, for it has many times been put to the test. Our soul therefore can, under the influence of a mysterious help always found to accompany deep desire, vitalize itself, so to speak, into what it used not to be.

How is it done? By being so enamored of moral beauty that we shall be indifferent to the admiration it cannot fail to bring forth. By absorption into it, or by absorption into some ideal which will only be an aspect of it. What is this, after all, if not the indifference to secondary forms of happiness which the Buddha, the Stoics, Fénelon and all the spiritual writers recommend? Not, by any means, indifference to our perfection, or to our happiness, but indifference to things which are of no value. Such a sense of self-realization accompanies this highly enlightened heroism that bliss is its reward.

Something else goes along with it: a certainty that by dedicating one's life to such a purpose one is collaborating with the Spirit and drawing as near to God as is possible for a creature originally made of clay. But this is the basic thought underlying every line of this book.

CHAPTER V

Technique

Words have their peculiarities, like people. We are shy of the word technical, but we read something attractive into the word technique. We imagine a technique as something infallible, not exceptionally difficult to learn, and working easily and smoothly. But more attractive than all others the technique of the spiritual life seems to be. There lingers about it a memory of the "mysteries" of old, with the hope of an initiation. Sometimes people ask about those methods in a guarded, almost insidious tone, as if the answers were sure to be reticent and it was not good form to be too direct about them.

As a matter of fact they are simplicity itself, and have been invented and re-invented again, expounded, discussed, clarified, expanded or contracted in so many ways that the literature about them fills libraries. Yet, what is really vital about them can be said in a few words.

The previous chapter makes it evident that what is intended is first the transformation of a man's mind, and second, the transformation of his life, his actions.

The transformation of the mind, in this case, has —except indirectly—nothing in common with intellectual progress as we generally understand it. It is immediately co-ordinated with our life, our emotions, our resolves and behavior. We endeavor to change our views because we feel a craving to become different people. This, properly analyzed, means that we are anxious to secure motive images which will make us more worth while than we were.

Somebody, for instance, notices with disgust that for several years his mind has been full of little else than the desire to imitate, and if possible surpass, a brilliant worldling whose polish, wit and apparent superiority to life have fascinated him. One day he reflects that, after all, should he succeed in this undertaking he would only be another object of envy to people similar to himself. As he is conscious of his inferiority to his model he is compelled to translate his state of mind into some admission like the following: I am trying hard to be admired by inferior people. Instantly the motive image of the fascinating worldling is weakened, while a craving for another image is born.

How can this new image be produced? Evidently the ordinary methods of culture can be resorted to. If the person in question reads history, he will meet characters remarkable for substance and manliness, yet quite as brilliantly fascinating as the one to whom he has just said good-bye. Alexander Hamilton, for instance. Another effort will substitute pure moral greatness for distinction, whereupon the name of Channing may replace that of Hamilton. One more effort, and the level of the great religionists will have been reached, with pure delight in collaborating with God and as complete an indifference to self as is possible to human frailty.

The images are not always personal or historical. A haunting thought of great power may be produced by casually going over a report of the situation of a stricken region, or of an orphaned family, perhaps by a few details concerning the white slave trade, or something similar. A man may never forget the beseeching eyes of a lost and starving dog and have his life changed by the recollection. Whatever the occasion may be, all the resources of the soul can be taxed by the presence of one image and a whole character can be transformed by it. Personal experience, of course, is more powerful than any book to produce such images, but, in default of it, books must be resorted to. Hence the importance which all wisdom methods attach to literature likely to invigorate instead of just amuse. Hence also the seriousness with which spiritual directors speak of reading. The word, as they use it, meaning special books, a special hour and special dispositions for the exercise, is so different from what we generally imagine that one feels like bracketing it.

"Special books, I admit. A particular hour may also be advisable. But what special dispositions can be necessary for that 'reading'. Is not attention enough?"

"No. Books to be read during the 'reading' hour, or half hour, or quarter of an hour, are not for our absorption. On the contrary, we should allow ourselves to be absorbed, not only in the book, but *by* the book."

"How can there be reading worth the name without the criticalness which you are constantly recommending?"

"To what extent are you critical when you listen

to Wagner, or read Keats? We should go to the spiritual authors we believe in as we go to poets or to nature: in order to grow. You may disagree with the wisest writer about peculiar issues, but you cannot disagree with his general rhythm, because it is the support of his deepest thought. I don't suppose you ever heard the name of Scaramelli, though he has been famous since the seventeenth century and is still read and respected. Well, Scaramelli's volumes are full of Teniers-like deviltries which even an Italian navvy needs no criticalness to disbelieve: he takes them for what they are: naïve legends or even apologues. His attitude is very much what Renan's used to be when he read the *Golden Legend*. The reader gets steeped in the rich atmosphere. Reading in that way is almost creative, for we give as much as the author gives us."

How else can we transform our mentality with a view to transforming our life? By the practise which most people identify with the fundamental occupation of wisdom schools, viz., meditation. The name alone has a virtue, for meditation is regarded by some as a superior reverie, by others as the proof of mental power, and, in both cases, it has charm.

What exactly is meditation? Meditation is not reading, no matter how reflective. Stop in front of a religious book-shop: you will see dozens of "manuals of meditation". Some of them are devoted to the *drill* of meditation and are as valuable to the psychologist as to the person who buys them to learn the principles of a real art. Many others sum up those precepts in a few pages and then proceed to give the reader short abstracts which he is supposed to expand by meditating upon them. You recognize a familiar school exercise. To the tyro in the art of meditating as to the student this exercise may be useful, it may also be the reverse. It is useful if the abstracts happen to be at one with the deeper tendencies of his mind, not so if they are foreign or contrary to them. I remember ridiculous abstracts the very subjects of which I should dislike to mention. But whether useful or injurious, this kind of meditation is only meditation by a misnomer: it is merely attentive reading.

Meditation is not the infinitely superior state of consciousness which we see described in the writings of the mystics either. That condition can best be realized by people who have had some experience of poetic inspiration, or upon whom nature acts in an irresistible way, or who are "not themselves" when they hear music. Such a beginning of ecstasy is evidently above anything that has a right to be called meditation.

Meditation is a contented, but perfectly conscious, dwelling of the mind on something likely to elevate our life. Here we are once more before a motive image, whatever its nature may be. If a Cambridge theological student who has just read Channing's *Life,* or his *Letters,* and has been impressed by the rare nobility of the man, goes down solemn Brattle Street thinking about him, and feeling all the time that he would love to devote his own life to great national or ethical objects, he is meditating. The magnetic spot in his life is before him, and he gives himself up to its attraction. Of course he is conscious all the time of how much help he is deriving from such a thought, and this consciousness brings him to the very border of prayer. In fact, if he is at all religiously-minded he will not be able not to pray. Only his prayer will be wordless and as vital as prayer can ever be made. The original Channing image may breed innumerable secondary images which will have a similar effect and may be connected with biographical developments of the young man by which they will be influenced, or which will influence them in return. All those images will produce meditations, and they will produce them at any time, or all the time. For people strongly impressed by one image are conscious, or semi-conscious of it, all the time.

"But do not people at wisdom schools meditate at certain hours?"

"Yes, and when they are possessed of a vital spiritual interest they look forward with irrepressible eagerness to those quiet intervals."

"Is it not better to meditate early in the morning?"

"If you are not dull or sleepy at those hours it certainly is a fine beginning of the day. But if your mind works best at night, when everything is quiet, you will find that your evening meditation will go on in your sleep and you will actually be meditating when you wake up. A French idiom speaks of 'morning people' and 'evening people'. The morning has a special virtue, like all newborn things, but evening is the poet's hour and Christ's day began at night, remember."

"What is a retreat?"

"A retreat is a return to, or a prolongation of, meditation. When an intellectual person feels stale, he goes away by himself to a quiet forest or fishing place, and he stays there till he feels fresh again. A retreat is a week's enjoyment of such a rest with thoughts we know to be helpful. The more we enjoy that spell the more useful it is. But even if it is partly mechanical or unwelcome it produces good effects. Silence always does."

"But if I have no motive images to attract me? . . . I shall be horribly bored."

"You certainly will. However, the case is far from being hopeless. If you have the faintest wish of seeing yourself living by yourself and thinking about your better self, *there* is your motive image. Play with it as long as you please, noting whatever serious thoughts may occur to you as you do so. The germ of your higher life cannot but be born in that way, for the wish for perfection is natural to us, and the quickness of its growth may be surprising to you."

So much for the technique of mind-transformation. There is also a technique of life-transformation the chief elements of which are called:

1. the ennobling of our intentions;
2. increasing our energy by a regulated life;
3. the spiritual fight or struggle with our faults; and
4. conscience-examination.

Here again psychological analysis will show us that this so-called technique is perfectly natural and simple. We carry it on unconsciously through our whole life, the moment we earnestly wish to secure some spiritual object.

The earnest wish is, of course, a necessity. Many people spend their lives wishing that they may wish enough to rise to a volition. But the volition remains only a wish. Those people dream of a higher life, as they dream of a more splendid destiny or of a larger fortune: the interior vision delights them and they are satisfied with that. In the same way you see men and women of a literary turn hoping, all their lives, that they may write books, but going on merely reading books: they are amused, but deceived and weakened by a mirage. Often, too, the impression left by some striking biography is too strong: we take it literally and we wait for impossible chances to reproduce its chief incidents. All this means dallying with a pleasing but indefinite image. The moment the image becomes clear, it also becomes imperative, for just as the chance for a noble action compels us to think nobly, a great ideal refuses to go back to the region of dreams.

The first thing to attend to is our thoughts. They naturally follow our desires, and, most of our desires being connected with ourselves, the thoughts will be selfish. We are willing to get rid of a glaring fault or two, but it will be in order to be admired the more. We easily go out of our way to do a good turn even to a stranger, but it is because we expect to make a friend of him, or merely because kindness is in the air and hoggism is not the fashion. The first step should be to correct that bend of our nature by learning to be disinterested in our thoughts. How is it done? Exactly as we change our bodily position from too much abandon to our grandmother's erectness. We all know how to get rid of an unpleasant thought; the same flexibility of mind which we acquire by repeatedly doing it is what is wanted to elevate our object in acting.

If we learn how to conquer ourselves in this invisible way, we shall find no great difficulty in extending the habit to outward circumstances. Our will-power, like all our faculties, resembles a muscle which exercise cannot but make stronger. Most people will find it necessary to subject their own life to regularity by adopting a routine. Office-life cannot go on without a schedule and discipline: camp-life is unthinkable without it. We must have some idea of when we want to get up or go to bed. We must "sometimes see", as harmonious Jeremy Taylor says in his longish *Rule of Holy Living,* "the sun get out of his chambers in the East", but we must not see him too often on our way back from social parties. We must have some idea of when we want to read that favorite book of ours, or when we want to be by ourselves to descend into silence. Of course if you attach too much importance to your schedule because it is *your* schedule, you will pay the penalty, for the schedule will become a fetish. But if you have no schedule at all you will do what you please, and no amount of doing that can fortify anything in us except a habit of seeking the easiest in everything.

Along with a regular life almost inevitably comes a desire to make the most of our life. Perhaps modern people, with the obsession of speed and the corresponding obsession of the brevity of time upon them, know that desire better than previous generations did. They indulge it in activity and nothing can be more legitimate. But our leisurely forbears were more inclined to devote themselves to their own improvement, whether it was through culture, or through elegance, or through devotion. The notion of getting rid of faults which they felt were in the way of their progress on any of those paths was familiar. Read the letters of that absolute worldling, Lord Chesterfield. Read, above all, the autobiography of Benjamin Franklin. These books are full of the notion that faults must be corrected. Now, there is only one way of getting rid of one's faults and that is to acquire the habits contradictory to them. We have a curious dread of the word habit when it connotes something we would like to secure. It seems to mean many months or years of effort, whereas we think that bad habits can be strongly planted in us in a few weeks. The idea creates a phantasm which is responsible for our worst error in soul-tactics, viz., putting off beginning. You know you bore or irritate people by endlessly talking about yourself and you want to get rid of the habit. Begin now, the moment you shut up this book. But do not say: I will never talk about myself any more. Say: I will never talk about myself any more in so-and-so's house, or on Mondays, or between six and seven o'clock. This limitation of one's effort, familiar to all psychologists, not only has made many people better company than they were, but it has increased their self-control and their self-confidence in an unexpected degree.

Conscience-examination is the corresponding practise. Franklin was familiar with it. He gives samples of charts on which he would report his delinquencies. Had he lived to-day, he would have completed those charts by a curve of progress or downfall. The most stubborn habits will not resist such a patient reiteration of resolve and control. But there must be a beginning and there must be reiteration, and control. There must also be good humor and a certainty that no Rome was ever built in a day.

Such is the drill or technique of soul-transformation. Psychologists have added variants to it and changed its vocabulary. The foundation remains what it used to be, and I have never opened a single ascetic book without marvelling at its simplicity.

CHAPTER VI

Wisdom Schools

CAN we retain our ideal and go on with the work of our improvement even in uncongenial surroundings? Many people think it impossible. As long as the company they cannot avoid, the books they imagine they have to read, and the circumstances they have to face are not likely to encourage the higher life, they think it useless to try. This notion is responsible for innumerable failures because it cuts at the very root of effort. When people, entirely at the mercy of their nerves and imagination, hear of artists and thinkers living together at Provincetown in search of a common ideal, they sigh. In such a milieu, they think, success would be easy and effort would become a pleasure. Unfortunately, only the happy few can break away from where destiny keeps them in chains.

Illusions! Success is never easy and labor is seldom delightful. Perhaps the people who fail in everyday surroundings would also fail in a wisdom school. But it is useless to speculate about might-be's. The plain truth is that a number of men and women manage to live the higher life in the midst of agitation and affairs. Think of Saint Paul, the vagrant contemplative. Think of Saint Bernard, leader and orator, and yet monk. Solitude was where those men were. Cannot we read also on the brow of many American business men turned philanthropists the kind of interior life which keeps them above their surroundings? No wisdom school, no cloistered seclusion is necessary for them. A man like the Apostle Paul was so full of one dominant purpose that he had no reason to fear company. Whenever a chance offered itself he spoke indefatigably of that with which his mind was overflowing. Seclusion must have been difficult in a city like Athens, but Socrates did not care: twenty people around him could not distract him from his thoughts. All men saved from the scattering influences of society by a powerful incentive, a cause, or an ideal of individual perfection, seldom fear the danger of being distracted by comers and goers.

Not so the average person who admires them, would like to imitate them, often thinks of doing so and honestly does his best, but frequently gets beaten because his inner fountain dries up the moment it is not sheltered. For such a man protection is necessary, and protection can only be solitude peopled by congenial companions. Hence the attraction of the ancient schools of philosophy, of Port-Royal, or to-day of such places as the Wisdom School at Darmstadt, or the Abbey of Pontigny when summer brings back to it its philosophers. Hence the popularity of the reading parties of Oxford, or the spiritual retreats given in hundreds of places. What attracts to the American Universities the men and women who go there for something else than a none too exciting salary? Clearly the hope of finding congenial company when solitude begins to pall, or conversely. Why are we conscious of self-collectedness much more than of dispersion when we meet the staffs of some high-class periodicals? Ideas work that miracle.

Monasteries are not for the very strong either, I mean not for men and women who feel in themselves the vocation and capacity for being leaders. They are for people who need and want a barrier between the world and themselves, or whose appetite for sacrifice can only be satisfied by anonymity, silence, obedience and penance rewarded by contemplation.

The chief object of Monasteries and Wisdom Schools has always seemed to me, first, to make spiritual progress easy for those who live there, that goes without saying, but also to remind outsiders that there is such a thing as spiritual progress whose attraction entices thousands and thousands from their occupations to leave them face to face with their thoughts. Who has ever been able to visit one of those retreats without being conscious, even in spite of prejudices, of a charm growing upon him? Who has ever left it without wistfulness? Ten or twelve miles from where I am now writing the slender spire of a Trappist monastery rises above the paling roofs of the conventual buildings. Why do I so often see in my mind's eye that abode of eternally silent monks? I could never be a Trappist, myself, I never thought of being one, never wished I was one. Yet, my summer ride seldom takes me in the direction of Scourmont without my feeling a keen desire to revisit the fields where those white or brown-robed men must now be making their harvest without ever a syllable. I know I could not speak to any of them. I do not like their psalmody which never dares to rise to a chant. But all the time I know that the religious spark which has made my life worth living rises to a bright flame in that community. Imagine the disappearance of the innumerable monasteries still subsisting on our incongruous earth, or that of their secular imitations. At once the many men and women who, unknown to one another, try to live up to their highest ambitions, would lose their bond, and, as it were, their banner. The thought of those privileged lives makes spiritual drudgery easier, as the thought of a metropolitan salon keeps alive a provincial artist's ambition. Effort, deprived of that help, would be condemned to cheerless individualism. The whole world would be a loser, as it would be if the Académie Française, or the Berlin Academy of Sciences, or Bayreuth suddenly became things of the past. Yet people who have never seen a monastery seldom speak of the monastic life charitably. Selfish life, they go on repeating, sometimes with perceptible irritation; monks live for themselves.

"Why, they do live a selfish life. Those people only think of themselves."

"They are happy. It should be enough for a generation which places happiness before everything else. Moreover, as William James tells us, quoting Hermann de Lorraine—one of them—they rather resent their own happiness and punish themselves ruthlessly for it. But monks and nuns, apart from exceptions, to which we shall soon revert, think of a great deal besides themselves. You could not say the same thing of a painter or sculptor in an artists' colony who only thinks of his gift."

"Yes, but the artist has a wife and children."

"Has he? And you want everybody to be happy

through a wife and children . . . Why should we force our formula of happiness on other people who may sue us for pernicious advice? Why always be dictatorially kind to outsiders who ask nothing of us? Yet, you never started a campaign against the New York bachelors so happy in their clubs 'where women cease to trouble'."

"I do not like them either."

"Too happy? or not happy enough? Let alone people's happiness, believe me, or let them arrange for their own happiness alone. What matters is what people count for."

"But monks and nuns who do not teach or do not do hospital work ought not to count. They are useless."

"You mean that contemplative religious are not useful in the ordinary sense of the word. You remind me of a debate I once followed on one of the French liners. A party of French engineers, on their way to America and full in advance of American practicalness, asked a Benedictine abbot on board to give them a talk on the utility of contemplative orders. The tall, handsome, dignified prelate talked on that subject for quite an hour and set the whole scholastic machinery in motion to leave no point undemonstrated. Still the engineers sat blank, polite but unconvinced. Their notion of utility was too definite to admit of anything contemplative, artistic or poetic. There they sat, hoping that the abbot might finally satisfy them, but luncheon became imminent and the debate threatened to be endless when I asked permission to intrude. 'I am afraid', I said, 'that the question you have been debating was in its very terms, misleading. No effort of dialectics can ever make contemplatives appear useful in the sense familiar to these gentlemen, except insomuch as they happen to wash up dishes or stoke the furnace. Contemplatives are not useful, they are only indispensable'.

"The Engineers stared more than ever.

"'Do you imagine', I went on, 'that the technically useful religious, those who do hospital work, for instance, would do it with the smile and in the spirit which ravished the Lutheran author of *The Story of San Michele* if they did not have special hours set apart for what is nothing else than contemplative meditation? They would be nurses, that's all. And do you suppose that their meditation could be what it is if there were no specialists to carry on a tradition which, without them, would inevitably be lost? It is another case of feeding the mother in order to make the baby strong. To change the simile to one nearer the subject, contemplation is the subtly burning tip of the flame lighting the world. Press it down and the light will smoke'.

"I had the satisfaction to find that this point of view could appeal even to industrialists. Not immediately, however, because the word utility had, in the course of the debate, become charged with more obstinacy than sense. But later in the day it was evident that these men realized how inevitable it must be that hospital nuns would lose in utility the moment they lost in radiation, and their radiation must be proportioned to their spiritual life."

If monasteries and wisdom schools were nothing else than great thoughts they would serve their purpose.

CHAPTER VII

Danger of Methodicalness

WARM, rich, generous natures have nothing to fear from rules and control. No regulations can make them narrow, no conscience-examination can make them over-conscious of themselves. They have faults which they know well; when they are taxed with them, their simplicity in admitting their existence disarms criticism. Their tone recalls the unfathomable sweetness of Hamlet's petition:

> "Nymph, in thy orisons
> Be my sins remembered."

Even when they are soaked in spirituality there is in them something human which breaks forth in sympathy or humor. No self-improved fetters can cramp such people. Healthy, well-balanced men and women also have everything to gain and nothing to lose by regulating and watching their lives. Wisdom books seem to have been written purposely for them. They understand every word of them and misunderstand nothing. If they discover any exaggeration in their ideas, they are on their guard against it, but they show no mean satisfaction at being right when the writer is wrong. When they are beaten by their faults they do not get discouraged. When they conquer them they praise the method they have used. Equilibrium is as enviable as great gifts and almost as exceptional.

Innumerable people are at fault in their judgments because of their vanity, which distorts everything. Quite as many make mistakes in their appreciation of themselves or of others because they are over-imaginative or over-sensitive. Lack of proportion is apt to make them ridiculously confident or, on the contrary, miserably diffident. The latter, during the nervous nineteenth century, used to be an immense army, and, in spite of the sanity which a better hygiene and a better spirituality are gradually holding up as a prerequisite to soul-growth, there are still thousands of them.

For such people a strictly regulated life accompanied by a reasonable concentration on themselves and on their faults need a counterweight which will be dealt with in the forthcoming chapters. Otherwise the results of even the best methods for moral improvement can be poor or worse than poor. Methods will make people methodical, and while it is a joy to deal with such people because one's life is never disarranged by their whims, everybody knows that not a few who adopt a method for the profit they expect from it gradually become so hypnotized by the method itself that they forget its object. Most people who use machinery thus become its victims. The same is true of collectors: at first they hunt specimens to demonstrate something; in time they do so merely to make their collection complete. Crankiness also waylays card-indexers: at their death, a houseful of cards will be found, but no result will have been produced. System which is only system is injurious to the mind.

Danger is not far either when meditation, which ought to be the fostering of an ideal destined to transform our life, degenerates into brooding on one's self, or when too much conscience-examination creeps into it. This habit weakens the power of the parent image which at first communicated its energy to the soul, and the object in view is missed. A person who is aiming to avoid ordinariness will only be distant or affected. He wanted to be superior in order to be influential, that is to say, useful: he will forget that ultimate goal and his distinction will only be food for his vanity. Our personal perfection becomes tainted with egotism the moment it ceases to be the means of other people's improvement.

Recollection, thoughtfulness, self-control often make people not only powerful but lovable. We realize that all the energy they store up by thus living within themselves is at our service. When we feel that it is not so, and are warned by infinitesimal but unmistakable signs that spiritual miserliness, instead of generosity, is at work, we know what to expect. The man we observe may have the gravity of many saints, he will never have their suavity. He will be self-contained and unsociable, mistrustful, under pretence of being on his guard against the world, and he will be dry and testy. No saint was ever disagreeable, but who can deny that when worldly people ask their question: why are pious people disagreeable? they have some reasons for asking it. The great stumbling-block of the frivolous lies there.

Should this perversion of a thing admirable in itself be charged to egotism, to human frailty or to the method employed? Certainly not to the method, which is often seen to work admirably. Not infrequently to egotism which is not difficult to detect. Ask the person whom you suspect of selfishness to contribute some of his time, or especially of his money to any good work you may be interested in. The degree of his acquiescence or hesitancy, other things being equal, will indicate that of his charity or egoism. But while we should be constantly watchful lest the care of our perfection should degenerate into concentration on ourselves, we should not be too hard on people who have partly succeeded in being pious without completely succeeding in being selfless. It is a strange tendency that some people have to make religion responsible for the egotism it has not been powerful enough to eradicate. We tolerate, sometimes admire selfishness in the statesman, the leader, the general, the philosopher or the artist, and we constantly make the mistake of attributing their greatness to that instead of to their genius: we listen without surprise, or without a word of blame, to a friend who tells us that the psychoanalyst has done wonders for him by advising him to sacrifice a near relation or a dear friend to his own "enrichment", but there is nothing we resent so much as the survival of egoism in religious people. Unfair. If we could be sure that by sacrificing their spiritual exercises these people could become sociable and charitable there would be some reason for our attitude, but we have no such certainty. Frailty, the everlasting deficiency of our nature is what is to be blamed for the apparent failure of spiritual methods. You may read with surprise Fénelon's admission: "I am for ever in quest of myself and turning around myself; languor is my reward."

"*What!*" you will exclaim, "*even a Fénelon the victim of too much self-examination! Self-examination cannot be good.*" A rash inference. Fénelon was a high-strung person who never cured himself of restlessness. Had he not patiently counteracted it through spiritual exercises he would not have left behind him a memory which everybody respects. He was by birth and disposition an ambitious man, aiming at the very highest posts in Church and State. In the semi-banishment of Cambrai, he might have brooded on injustice and died in bitterness instead of developing the exquisite gentleness for which he is famous. Soul-culture saved him.

Thoughtlessness may easily saddle on spiritual technique worse consequences than even egotism or morbidity. Count Keyserling plaintively says somewhere that philosophy has made his mind and soul so malleable that he can hardly call them his soul and mind any more—a complaint of all men and women whose thoughts and emotions perpetual handling has made as flexible as clay. They look back with regret to the days when their soul, being less obedient, was more resilient. Yet, what they have lost by acquiring this fluidity is nothing to what a host of noble souls have been deprived of by suicidal doctrines like Buddhism in its extreme form, Marcionism, Calvinism, or its Catholic counterpart Jansenism. Buddhism openly and unhesitatingly leads its best adherents to annihilation. Marcionism hated all that made for life. Its initiator, a brilliant convert of the second century, may have been long dead, but his spirit—which made voluntary death by starvation a pious deed for the Cathares of the twelfth century—is still alive in an exaggerated abhorrence of matter more frequent than people imagine. The dogma of joylessness is, of course, the foundation of Calvinism and Jansenism. Both doctrines no sooner appeared than they were condemned by the Church, but their founders had in them the kind of strength which can not be disposed of by censures. Open at random some one of the many spiritual books written in French or Italian in the seventeenth century, you will find traces of Jansenism on every page, in the language, in the very rhythm. What devotional book to-day would dare to speak of Christ—Christ, not Jehovah—as an "angry judge"? Yet, the phrase was common in those days. Fear of damnation, fear of wasting spiritual chances, fear of not listening to the call of perfection was almost universal and was not checked as it is to-day by a completely different atmosphere. However, the gospel of fear is not entirely forgotten. How many English or American writers, brought up in calvinistic homes, have not had the same tale to tell as Edmund Gosse? Was not religion, until recently, too often presented as inimical to joy? Only a few years ago, in dusty Glasgow, a smiling nun, with a twinkle in her eye, told me that the day before, the school-inspector having called and conscientiously gone through his dreary duties, she suggested a cup of tea and a piece of newly-baked cake "which would gladden his heart".—"We should not be happy, Sister," was the tart answer.

This, of course, happened in Glasgow, but the spirit of old Knox travels.

The early Christians would have been astounded at the manifestation of such a spirit. To them salvation only meant regret for one's past and belief that Jesus was the Son of God. After that, *agallasis,* or alacrity, was the word. The teaching of the Church has always been marked by sanity. This not only appears in her condemnation of the life-poisoning doctrines recalled above, but in her liturgy, and in her practise. Instead of praying for trials, the Church, like Israel before her, prays for peace and prosperity. And assuredly the cathedrals would not be what they are, lyrical invitations to soaring above earthly misery, the music we hear there would not have its celestial quality, if Christian beliefs were to darken our whole existence. The reaction against Calvinism is now evident in the hedonism which clamors in all the manifestations of modern life, but it is equally visible in the tone, attitude and devotions of the Church since the seventeenth century. What is now called "benedictine piety", a spirit of simple and happy union with God with no immediate thought of consequent moralism, is the Church's farewell to what still survived of Jansenism thirty or forty years ago.

In spite of this transformation there will always subsist the danger of a narrow outlook and of egotistical concentration in any technique of self-improvement based on unguided meditation and short-sighted conscience-examination. The individual becomes too conscious of himself to be easily detached from himself.

CONCLUSION OF THE PREVIOUS CHAPTERS

There is in the world, there is even in spiritually inclined people, such a rankling irritation against joy-killing puritanism that many readers will be more affected by the foregoing chapter than by the six that came before it. The inward questions: Can't we be ourselves? Can't we live our poor little life in peace? must have been heard more or less distinctly in many a consciousness as the ghost of old-fashioned rigor floated through these pages. Unbearable, hypocritical, selfish must have been epithets ready at hand for defence.

But, is it possible that the pursuit of moral beauty should be productive of results so unlike beauty? Is it possible that a man whose soul is warmed and brightened by an ideal should look like an eighteenth century Massachusetts deacon? that sadness should be the share of those who want more perfection in themselves that there may also be more in the world?

The following chapters will show that we can regulate our lives and yet be natural, that we can love without being diminished by love, and finally that we can gain more than lose by breaking away from ourselves to indulge in activity. There are a hundred ways of doing the same thing: the spirit in which it is done alone matters.

CHAPTER VIII

Naturalness

NATURALNESS is a form of sincerity, and, in consequence, needs no vindication. One can be natural while regulating one's life, watching one's impulses, or keeping one's faults under control, as one can be natural while singing according to principles. Only your inferior artist looks tortured when he tries to remember his technique.

We have a perfect right to let others see us as we really are. But we must be careful not to over-emphasize our frankness. Anglo-Saxons are more sincere than they are natural because they are apt so to over-emphasize. Many Latins, like myself, will never forget what they owe to English or American sincerity. The absolute freedom, the transparency of such a psychological document as the correspondence of Katherine Mansfield acts on French people as a revelation. Yet English people are often not natural because they are self-conscious, and Americans because they are exaggeratedly effusive. People ask: what is there more natural than being natural? but the question would not be asked by a psychologist who knows that he is not himself without a certain amount of self-surveillance.

The most frequent mistake is to imagine that one is more natural by letting other people see one's faults than by letting them see one's qualities. This fallacy is the offspring of the other illusion: "one man is as good as another", from which is born the certainty that one is infallible. With such a psychological background one can say everything, if not do everything, and feel above all danger of blame or entirely indifferent to it. But all the time there will lurk, almost imperceptible in the consciousness of the person who thus squanders himself, a desire to get rid of the very faults he is displaying with so much complacency, and when the conversation is over, a dissatisfaction with himself. We should not speak of ourselves oftener than real aristocrats speak of their ancestry, and when we allude to our shortcomings it should be in the tone of Jean-Baptiste Vianney when he referred to his "poor sins", and not with the suppressed elation of self-admiration.

Most of the dangers besetting a narrowly regulated life come from missing the relative importance of things. Some people imagine they cannot be right at a quarter to eleven if their schedule decides that it should be at eleven o'clock sharp. Such slavish literalness can only come from stupidity or mania. In the same way trifles will be resented as much as serious offences. No Frenchman as near spiritual greatness as Richard Froude was would ever yawn a semi-cynical remark while stretching himself on a sofa. The abandon of the attitude shocks him. But a mere attitude has nothing to do either with the truth of a remark or with the moral distinction of the person who utters it. It is as foolish to think that a sofa is incompatible with a lofty ideal, like

Froude's, as to think that yawning and stretching are proofs of naturalness. Being natural consists in neither concealing nor displaying one's ideal, and in acting directly in accordance with what it dictates.

This remark leads us to the relation existing between a man's naturalness and the images he obeys. The more powerful a motive image is the more play it leaves to naturalness. Great men are almost invariably as natural as children, because, their attention being concentrated on the one object all-important in their lives, all the rest seems immaterial to them. I have seen people stare in pained astonishment at Saint Paul's reference to his quarrel with a blacksmith. To me this simplicity is only a proof of the human greatness of Paul. Imagine any of our contemporaries alluding to some feud with a garage man. But you can easily imagine a whole-souled man like Shakespeare doing it, because from the height where he would stand all humans must seem simply human to him.

On the whole, the measure of the freedom we can allow ourselves in speaking or acting is the extent to which this freedom can affect our ideal or that of the people who depend on our example. Within these limits naturalness is a right, and restraint brings the danger of becoming morbid.

CHAPTER IX

The Culture of Feeling

MAN is an eolian harp. As long as he does not allow himself to be paralyzed by habit, that is to say thoughtlessness, or hardened by interest or self-defence, or annihilated by imitation, he does not think of himself as living in the world but as being part of the world. Children feel this so strongly that they are inclined to regard their consciousness as a delusion. As for men and women who manage to retain the impressionability of childhood after acquiring the grown-up capacity for conscious reactions, they seem to live in a state of perpetual vibration. Open at random any one of the great poets, you will notice that the spiritual exchange between them and the world is continuous. Nature of course is the nearest to us. She is so near and dear that we call her maternal and never feel that the epithet is an exaggeration. Her power is obvious in the great scenes which the ocean, the mountains or the forests offer us, but it seems the most striking in this: whenever, in an hour of reverie, we slide back to our farthest-away memories, we almost invariably find ourselves re-living some apparently trivial incident. After years of forgetfulness we see ourselves standing before a bit of hedge, entranced by the rich reds of the hips and haws set off by the luscious black of elder-berries. Or we seem to hear a far-away church-clock which we did not suspect of having left such an echo in our soul. Sometimes the memory of a flower, a humble floweret on a bank, will be enough to ravish us. Sometimes the mere name of that flower will act upon us as if it were a poem. The spell of nature would be inexplicable if we did not remember that our origin actually makes us part of it.

There is something else than mere charm or sensuousness about this spell: it possesses a virtue. No man ever likes to be roused out of one of those exquisite moods by the mention of a sordid detail in his everyday life. None can pass from it to a mean action. Nature never produces anything ignoble.

Much the same rare and elevating charm is attached to our enjoyment of far-away places, especially with historic or romantic associations. We feel different after an hour not only before the Parthenon which epitomizes beauty, but before the Colosseum which has only solemnity, or in the quaint streets of Perugia. The moment we are plunged in the consciousness of the past we feel a new sense of continuousness in our own life. Instead of nursing petty personal grievances we espouse the cause of a nation, and our little chronicle rises to the level of history.

Even the mere sensation of being far away from home is enough to wrench us out of our humdrum ordinariness. I can remember one late afternoon in the elegant but lonely avenues of Los Angeles which, ten or twelve years ago, still lost themselves in the druidical-looking fields where, without a single soul in sight, the oil-pumps kept up their dull automatic concert. The streets were poorly marked, and none of the few pedestrians I met knew even the name of the place I was looking for. Gradually the night closed in and brighter stars than Paris ever sees began to peer at me over the unfriendly Sierra. I felt far away from home, and the work I was engaged in at the time was anything but cheering. Yet that hour left on me an impression which I should be reluctant to lose and which I have, many times, revived. Anything rather than the comfortable uniformity of a sleepy existence.

"But my existence is *sleepy and has always been ordinary."*

"Has it? Do you ever take the trouble to look into it and give its incidents a chance? Many people, most people, live in the present and think it a waste to resuscitate the past. But the real waste is to leave untouched the store of experience which a human life is bound to accumulate. Our life originally was a venture. Would it be a success? and of what kind? We might have made wagers about it. At present, if we only look back, we can tell how much of it has answered our hopes, how much has been failure. We know to what extent we have secured happiness or piled up disappointments. Above all, we can easily tell how, through years of temptation and struggle, our early ideal has fared. Is it still the bright beacon it used to be? Is our ambition still to be the kind of person who attracts, or are we satisfied with drifting? This questioning may not be delightful, but it is certainly not boresome.

The memory of our joys, even of our sorrows, is another reserve on which we can draw. That joys never were merely good times our choice will immediately remind us. Before going back to our sorrows we may be more uncertain. The world has a habit, which it is only too ready to crystallize into a theory, to regard sorrow as a sin. It tells us to run away from it. There are well-known resorts, both in Europe and in America, which are sanctuaries against it or the memory of it. People who go there after the loss of a beloved one are declared "fine" when they laugh. Senseless cowardice. Triumph of inanity. No man strong and brave enough to have set his all on a hope, or a love, will ever condescend to brush aside disappointment or bereavement. Only people of weak minds or feeble hearts can thus shrug away sorrow.

"But sorrow can be morbid, and doctors forewarn against it."

"As they do against anything. Sorrow manfully braved and accepted can never be morbid and has, many times, been a fountain of nobility. Read Tennyson's *In Memoriam.* Whenever you see on a person's face that exceptional depth or gravity which even the soulless envy, be certain that the chisel of sorrow has cut those marks thus deep. Brave sadness does for us what winter does for the earth."

Quite as cowardly and, in the end, quite as injurious to our soul, is the fear of facing other people's suffering. It may torture my sensibility to read a report about famine, unemployment, or vivisection, but better be galvanized into action by excruciating knowledge than be kept in shameful peace by supineness. People who, every now and then, feel they must visit a hospital ward, people who cannot hear of a poor woman feeding stray animals without occasionally sending her a little money, people who do not like to see the flowers of the week consigned to the dust-bin and go out of their way to give them Ophelia's end on the cool river, people who cherish a fondness even for an old piece of furniture or a superannuated watch may seem exaggerated or even abnormal to so-called sane individuals of florid mien and merry approach, but how poor the world would be without them!

It would be useless to recall here the place which sympathy in its multitudinous forms occupies in our life. The next chapter will go into it more fully. Needless also to do more than mention the beautiful friendship between man and animal which ought to have a chapter in every treatise on happiness. But the manifestations of human sensibility are endless.

Life, real life, full life consists of a thousand impressions coming to us from every part of our moral horizon, accompanied sometimes by the warmth of admiration, sometimes by the reaction of activity. Readers of the Brownings have no doubt that even if these two remarkable individuals had never written a line their interior existences would, however, have been magnificent symphonies. Narrow or harness the stream of such lives and you will be undoing the work of God. Frame theories, or suggest soul-treatment intended to cramp the possible fullness of even much less gifted individuals and you will substitute a wooden frame for growth. Not a few suicidal schools have done so.

What such schools hold up as an ideal, specialists often practise without bothering about advocating it. They try to save their souls by renouncing the world, that is to say they protect their object by leaving out all that is not conducive to it. The specialty to which they are wedded makes them insensible to the rest, that is all. Dalton, the founder of atomic chemistry, a typical savant even more than a typical Quaker, shows us in an often-quoted letter a remarkable instance of this state of mind:

> "Being desired to call upon a widow—a Friend, who thought of entering her son at the academy—I went and was struck by the sight of the most perfect figure that ever human eyes beheld, in a plain but neat dress; her person, her features were engaging beyond all description. Upon enquiry I found she was universally allowed to be the handsomest woman in Manchester. Being invited by her to tea a few days after, along with a worthy man here, a public Friend, I should in any other circumstances have been highly pleased with an elegant tea equipage, American apples of the most delicious flavour, and choice wines; but, in the present, these were only secondary objects. Deeming myself, however, fully proof against mere beauty, and knowing that its concomitants are often ignorance and vanity, I was not under much apprehension. But she began to descant upon an exact acquaintance with English grammar and the art of letter-writing; to compare the merits of Johnson's and Sheridan's dictionaries; to converse upon the use of dephlogisticated marine acid in bleaching; upon the effects of opium upon the animal system, etc., etc. I was no longer able to hold out, but surrendered at discretion.
>
> "During my captivity which lasted about a

week, I lost my appetite and had other symptoms of bondage about me, as incoherent discourse, etc., but now have happily regained my freedom. Having now wrote till I have tired my hand and thine eyes, I shall conclude with my love to Cousin Ruth and thyself and to all enquiring friends."

What is the reaction of most people? Of course, they say that scientists are formulas and not human beings. We also know that, in their heart of hearts, they regard religion as cramping human nature, while critics, generalizing that impression, flatly declare religion irreconcilable with art.

But the following remarks should be made.

In the first place, the spiritual writers who narrow the channel of life under pretence of deepening it never belong to the great tradition of mystics who are closely related to poets and frequently find prose inadequate to the expression of their multitudinous souls. Almost invariably they are timid in thought and frigid in style. If the traditional drill of spiritual life did not give a borrowed value to their books they would appear in all their indigence and nobody would give a thought to their advice.

Contrast them with the Biblical writers, not as deformed and diluted in the old-fashioned, unnatural presentment, with its absurd division in verses, but as they appear in modern editions: poets, most of them, ardent national bards, or constantly mingling the spontaneous feelings of humanity with the consciousness of God's presence in the world. At once the so-called spiritual writers shrink into insignificance.

In the second place, these theorists of repression are at variance with the wholesomeness and sanity of the Church in her official teachings as well as in her liturgy and in her well-known attitude towards culture and art. Push their tendencies to their extreme logicalness and what will become of the world? They lack the insight necessary to understand the perfect naturalness of a Jeanne d'Arc, the passionate nature of a Paul, or what makes Christ a hero of his nation as well as the exemplar of humanity. In everything they show mediocrity often made touching by humility or the capacity for self-sacrifice, but sometimes positive and trenchant, and never lovable.

Finally, and this is the worst reproach they deserve, their idea of God would be blasphemous if they fully visualized its implications. The notion that God gives us all our emotional faculties merely to make a sacrifice of them to Him transforms the Deity into something worse than the jealous tribal God of the early Hebrews, a sort of Moloch. We shall have a chance to deal more fully with misconceptions of God through ignorance or thoughtlessness, but it is sufficient to recall here the line of the Greek poet Aratus, quoted with approval by the Apostle Paul:

> In God we live, and move, and we exist.

The ocean of Divinity in which we float is not affected by what our shrunken personality may do.

What we should conclude is that whatever in us does not thwart the divine plan is legitimate. Only, supreme in our existence, should prevail as noble an ideal as we are capable of, the kind of ideal which is not forced upon us from outside, but which being natural to us, spreads to all our actions, lends them its glow, and makes them more eloquent than words. That indeed is not merely what God wills in us, it is God in us. If such an ideal dominates our consciousness we shall know how to value all that comes in its train: our sensations, emotions, or inclinations. Abandonment to God's will—the everlasting motto of the ascetic—only means the duty of securing happiness by preferring something to nothing, or nobility to insignificance. That, indeed, is the will of God.

CHAPTER X

Love

THE most self-centered man, the most anxiously attentive to his interior life and the most visibly in danger of forgetting that perfection should take into account other people's perfection as well as one's own, cannot persevere in that condition the moment he experiences love. But another danger threatens him instantly, for his ideal runs the risk of being submerged by the violent and composite nature of his sentiment.

It is not an easy task to speak of love. It has the reputation of unsettling life. Bacon, in one of his essays, the cynical tone of which is not pleasant, and Saint Paul, in a sad tender passage of Corinthians I, take that view. On the other hand, nobody can give the subject a moment's thought without recognizing that love is an evident part of the divine plan and therefore can only be regarded as normal.

But here again there is danger. No word has been treated so unceremoniously by the past three or four generations as love has been. Modern literature in its delight at having broken loose from Puritanic restraint is vociferous in giving it its most technical and consequently its most inadequate meaning. The theatre and the lecture-platform resound with it till one is sick of its implications. On the other side, orthodox moralists who declare sexual relations "indifferent", that is to say neither good nor bad in their own nature, are however on their guard against them. The reason is that nowhere is use so much in danger of turning to abuse as it is here. Hence even the view taken of marriage is pessimistic. Madame de Maintenon, viewing it from the woman's standpoint, certainly regarded it as mute resignation to unwelcome demands. The notion of love in marriage seemed so exceptional as to be almost improper. Yet, there was an idea that marriage worked like magic to induce love even in innocent girls—"white geese"—who were pushed blindly into it.

Contradictions, on this subject, seem to be the rule, even among people who would be expected to know and whose confident tone leads one to imagine that they do know. The theorists in the smoking-room declare, in one breath, that love is supreme, in the next they say it is nothing. All this comes from the most usual cause of human error, viz., confusion of terms, so that there is nothing more imperative than to remind the human race that love is one thing, lust is another. If modern people would be as frank about this as they pretend to be they would resolutely adopt this vocabulary and cease to apply, to what is whispered about amid unpleasant chuckling, the word which poetry has glorified in a thousand forms. The world would at once be a better world because truth would force upon it realities instead of lies as the language does to-day. But the confusion will go on for some time. Modern daring is supposed to know no restraint and respect no conventionalities. In reality one need not observe it long before noticing that it is exactly as hypocritical as Victorianism at its worst used to be.

It must be admitted that even perfect sincerity is often baffled by the complexity of what we call love, that is to say sex-attraction in its most legitimate form. It has a physical aspect which no spiritualization can make other than it is. Without it the world would promptly come to an end, and both Church and State agree that, in its default, marriage is not complete and can be annulled as not answering its specific object. Indeed, the majority of mankind regards it as the one kind of magic to which all men have a right, while the strictest moralists recognize in it something higher than mere necessity. Perhaps things would be improved if the consciousness of the prevalent lowness of standards did not compel these moralists often to be silent about it, but human distortion is more to be blamed than their reticence. Silence is better than the affirmation so often repeated now-a-days that sexual urges are of exactly the same order as other physical impulses, and have the same right not only to be indulged but to be openly discussed.

In the first place, why should this particular tendency be discussed any more openly than others about which not a word is ever said? One of the most striking characteristics of a man who is really in love, is that his conversation is chaste. He is willing to analyze sentiment, but not sensation. When he begins to do so it is a sign of deterioration. In the second place, it is not true that the relations between the sexes are of the same order with the rest of man's instincts. They have social consequences which place them in a class apart. The Dutch dancer Mata-Hari was only the banal mistress of a French Cabinet

Minister during the war; but as she also was the mistress of the chief of the Berlin police the results were worse than those generally produced by such affairs: it is estimated that fifty thousand soldiers, humble men on the sanguinary chess-board, were sacrificed to the caprice of two personages comfortably out of danger. This is a magnified instance which needed a unique catastrophe to attain such proportions, but in every case love is productive of serious consequences, good or bad. Somebody is made happy, or, on the contrary, is made to suffer; somebody's freedom is aided or annihilated; somebody's life is enhanced or it is wasted: often children are born, and the perspective, instead of merely being idyllic or farcical, becomes dramatic. Nothing comparable happens in the other sections of our urges.

Individual consequences can be such that a man's or a woman's whole existence is affected by them. The wife or husband-complex is not a mere word. People are only mildly ridiculous and common when they wax enthusiastic in public over their "best husband" or their "little woman", but there are certainly married people whose individuality is destroyed by the exaggeration of their sentiment, by subtle fears of displeasing or misunderstanding, or merely by the proximity of a force out of proportion with their own. A union which was intended to fortify results in weakening. A blank expression, a mute docility, or the whipped-dog attitude replace spontaneity. Often insincerity can be detected.

Modern people think it their duty, or, through imitation, contract a habit, to exaggerate the expression of love, especially in their letters. Nobody is deceived by that style, but it is more and more widely adopted. What can be the results of straining one's expression in that way? Merely a fallacious expectation of what in one's heart one knows to be unreal. On the contrary, when we read such letters as those of Katherine Mansfield to her husband, we may be conscious of a certain exaggeration in the deliberate restraint, but we feel that this exaggeration was healthier than its opposite and must have produced freshness instead of unreality. The mushiness of the popular novel and, even more, of the cinema is primarily a lie.

This deterioration can happen to the individual even when his sentiment is what people call "nice". The moment it oversteps the boundary between love and sexual indulgence the deterioration becomes far worse. George Bernard Shaw, whose views on the subject are rigid and who, like Bacon, is not far from lowering love to a form of insanity, rightly observes that this can occur, and frequently does occur, in marriage which then becomes a deliberate legalization of sin. No matter how situated may be the person intemperate in that way, his punishment is inevitable.

In the first place he defeats his own object as intemperance always does. By concentrating on a single aspect of his sensory life he loses the subtle polyphony of which purer and truer love is so irresistibly conscious that it is almost afraid of it.

This cannot but lead to satiety which obviously is a form of dissatisfaction, but, as the urge subsists in a strengthened form, an obsession is created with a mere something replacing somebody. Don Juan is not a happy man. If he were he would not be Don Juan. And he is not a sane man either. Montaigne speaks with contempt of *l'homme dont la paillardise sans cesse régente la tête,* "the man whose head is a merry-go-round of lustful images". Don Juan is a neurotic and has a right to medical treatment.

In time he becomes like a miser, obsessed with the idea that he cannot afford to lose anything, and this belief in instability gives him a sort of mock stability, but he cannot but know that such a principle is only one more shadow in his pursuit of shadows.

He may have been seductive before becoming a seducer, temptations have often been in his way, and extenuating circumstances sometimes make him pathetic enough, but his weakness leads him to do things which he may naturally abhor. He is horribly and deliberately deceitful, he is inevitably cruel, and he cannot escape from the consciousness of a certain caddishness in his ways, or from the fear that clear-sighted people may read his real character.

When he is actually seen through, even by people in the same fraternity, he feels their contempt in the familiarity of their approval. He overhears suppressed laughter oftener than the expression of admiration for his performances. He knows he is regarded less as a successful pirate than as the comical prisoner who gets trapped in his own ambush.

From this sex obsession, thanks to which human beings are degraded to more or less colorful moments, love is free. Assuredly it cannot exist without a sensuous element. Sex attraction has to be based on visible things: beauty, the voice, the general deportment; moreover the more or less remote promise of fulfilment is not absent from its inception. But what is sensuous is not necessarily sensual. Love, as distinguished from desire, notices the face before the figure and the eyes before the features; it sees grace where passing admiration only bows to shapely forms, and it is conscious of the subtleties of charm, when they exist, under the sinuous lines of gracefulness. It listens more than it looks and analyzes as naturally as it feels. It registers innumerable nuances in tastes, notions, and tendencies which will be its life-long food after visible attractions have faded away. In short it is pre-eminently conscious of personality, and that must remain its characteristic even when physical union is included, for that consciousness is synonymous with preference, and without preference there is no love, but mere sexual impulses.

This preference must be exclusive, for a person who cannot tell which of two attractions is the stronger upon him is in great danger of soon being conscious not merely of two attractions but of twenty. It must also be independent of time and space. As Mrs. Browning says: unless you can love, as the angels may, with the breadth of heaven betwixt you, oh! fear to call it loving.

Often love is not entirely aware of itself, because admiration is so overpowering that it leaves it no time for self-analysis. There is no doubt, at present, that if ever a woman was in love with a man, Charlotte Brontë was in love with her professor at Brussels, Constantin Héger. But anybody who has studied the character and life of that complicated woman has no doubt that she did not know the nature of her sentiment and would have been indignant had it been called by its real name.

People with naturally refined natures will obviously be more likely to know real love than men and women of a coarser fibre, or merely of a more exuberant disposition. Chateaubriand, who had many experiences, undoubtedly knew less about love than his sensitive but exclusive friend, Joubert. I never can read without amusement a passage from M. Lanson's *History of French Literature* in which this famous scholar criticizes in Fénelon's *Télémaque* "a description of love by a priest who had no idea of love". As if sentiment, in all its forms, could be foreign to that perfection of sensibility, the Archbishop of Cambrai! Did Alcibiades, the rake, know more about love than Plato, or Horace more than Virgil? Why should fulfilment be necessary for the understanding of what conditions it, and is infinitely more dramatic than average physical love can ever be? Fénelon, a prince of charm and the incarnation of elegance, had spent the best part of his life at court, near its attractions, and probably near its temptations; he was the recipient of confidences of all kinds; why should he know less of love than if he had had the trivial experience which anybody can secure so cheaply?

"You only speak of romantic love?"

"No, I speak of love, plain love, but as distinguished from what is called love by writers who gravely assure us that one can be in love with a person one does not like. This extension to normal cases of psychological anomaly is the most extraordinary joke practised on uncritical mankind by inferior artists who know that ugliness is more easy to paint than beauty, and succeed in persuading the world that beauty should no longer be painted."

"But then, is not love so rare as hardly to exist at all?"

"It certainly is rare. The proof of this is that only a few men, like Abélard, Petrarch, or Michelangelo, have achieved a reputation as lovers, while most types of rare and exalted passion belong to imaginary literature. But comparative rarity does not mean impossibility. We need only look around us to see attachments the depth and beauty of which should be a lesson as well as an encouragement to mankind. I personally know whole groups not one member of which has made a failure of his love."

"Old-fashioned people?"

"Yes, every one of them. But you will notice that all happy people, no matter how brilliant, have an old-fashioned look about them. Cinema stars are no exceptions."

"Is there no happiness of the kind you mention outside of wedlock?"

"It would be absurd to say there was not. But even that happiness also seems what you call old-fashioned, because fulness creates repose. Besides, let it be pointed out that such couples invariably show two characteristics: they crave recognition, which is another name for marriage, and they long for children: real love always wants to proclaim and to perpetuate itself."

Probably the greatest mistake made by our modern world is to speak of love all the time, and to give the impression that love offers itself to every one all the time. As a matter of fact attraction is continuous, but love only comes once. Most people learn this as a conclusion of varied experiences. Too late. Few miss the encounter which shows them what their life might have been. The usefulness of the romantic drama lies in its emphasis on this uniqueness of love. The more romantic people are about this the nearer they are to truth.

It is because, in spite of certain appearances and in spite of current literature, this remains a dogma in American life that marriage in the United States is not, by any means, the failure that blatant exaggerations make it out to be. More than anywhere else, it is true, the life of young people in America resembles the wild turmoil of little birds on St. Valentine's Day. But under the love skirmishes which thus go on for a while is hidden the certainty that promiscuousness should never be more than an appearance. There is more of this same feeling than of an approximation to free love even in the melancholy admission of error that the American divorce is. The brazen declarations of a few professionals should not outweigh the sincere wish of many remarried *divorcés* that they had never been married before. I also doubt if there is another country in the world where so many patient Jacobs serve, through the long years, not unwilling Labans but dilatory Rachels. To a European recently arrived from the other side of the Atlantic these humble knights at first seem more ridiculous than touching. In time the visitor reconsiders his judgment and reads in this, as in so many other peculiarities, an evidence of American youthfulness.

For all young people instinctively precede their

soi-disant more experienced elders in the certainty that one's mate is not to be found by a random plunge into any inviting crowd. Many a prematurely grave young fellow is protected against inferior temptations by one radiant souvenir. Romanticism again, no doubt. But whoever looks for love cannot but encounter romanticism.

Literature, at least in the phase we are at present passing through, ignores this, or makes it loathsome by a cheap expression of sentiment which can never be literary, but the reason is not that pure love—in the sense in which we say pure poetry—is not literary. It is simply that it takes genius to write *Adolphe,* or *Wuthering Heights.* It is largely the lack of literary talent that is responsible for the universal and silly illusion that physical love has anything in common with the psychological paradises conjured up by the mere desire for it. The pessimism of many talented realists would be not only an absolute but a wholesome proof of this if it could only be less one-sided. If the average reader had mental energy enough to judge the pages he reads instead of floating along them, his views would promptly become sane and the so-called crisis of modern marriage would be reduced to the inevitable proportion of error in human decisions.

"Error, illusions. You are confronted with the inevitable realities at last. No matter how romantic, pure, or ultra-sensible our idea of love may be, men and women will make mistakes in their choices. And they will suffer in consequence."

Infinitely less than if they did not have that capital of high sentiment to start with. People are not blinded by romantic love, they are the victims of a magical trick practised by love. When love is real love, when people's souls go out to their beloved, when they lose their hearts to them, when they act in the unselfish way which these exquisite old English phrases denote, a miracle is produced. Without any effort, without the least hypocrisy, men and women only show their best as birds are at their most brilliant in April. It is difficult then to exercise one's critical faculties and not to "buy the cat in a bag", *acheter chat en poche,* as the French phrase goes. Yet, there is a brief period between attraction and fascination, during which wisdom still has her word to say. Then is the time to remember that the happiness of most people we know is not ruined by great catastrophes or fatal errors, but by the repetition of slowly destructive little things. Trivial pieces of egotism, a not very obvious but chronic habit of thoughtlessness, unexpected outbursts, an idea that politeness is a superfluity with the people one lives with all the time, result in the same barrenness of feeling that some violent reactions will produce. These warning incidents should be taken notice of and put under the microscope while it is not too late. If, while the May moon shines on the fragrant hay, you are ever so little offended by an "I—I—me—me" attitude, multiply your annoyance by a hundred and decide whether you can endure it in future. Discount sex appeal as much as you can, and try to remember the old saying that one should only let oneself fall in love with the woman who could be made a friend of if she were a man. Otherwise the inward note made by us all the time: "he or she has done this" will gradually change to "he or she *does* this" and inevitably, some day, the final and catastrophic "he or she *IS* this or that" will mark the end of the spell that love had been.

Such precautions should be elementary. If, instead of attaching so much importance to the so-called technique of love,—so obvious that its simplicity is offensive,—people would give the least attention to the morals or the minor morals of married life, they would be touching instead of so often being laughable in their disappointments, and, above all, their disappointments would be less frequent. But the lesson of experience is that mankind, all the time in quest of recipes for wisdom and happiness, does not see the obvious conditions of wisdom or happiness. The mortal sin of literature is to emphasize the difficulty, instead of the simplicity, of this common-sense view of life. On the other hand the folly of men and women is to imagine, when they read such simple advice, that it is enough to have read it, instead of starting out to live it. A minimum of sense would inevitably ensure that modicum of satisfaction which most humans regard as bliss.

To sum up, love is sure to bring down to solid earth people inclined to soar out of the stratum of realities. Only it should not make them terrestrial. If the higher companionship that love should be does not make men and women nobler, more generous, more ready to sacrifice even their beautiful life for a lofty purpose, there is a suspicion that their love is not love but a combination of egoisms. True love makes our ideal brighter and our purpose stronger. If the word God, with the train of superior thoughts and superior sentiments that it connotes, is only used with an awkward feeling by people who think themselves in love, let them be sure that they miss the best part of love, and not only of romantic love but of simply love. A glance at the writings of any one of the Platonists will make them realize that it is so. But if they are shy of those great connoisseurs in love, let them read between the lines of even the so-called revolutionary champions of "modern" love. They will discover that experimenting and tabulating brings those specialists to the self-same ideas set forth in this chapter. Perhaps the ignoble theorist of pleasure himself occasionally catches a glimpse of such notions, because they are so much more real than they are romantic.

George Sand, whose sentimental failures are well-known to every reader of the lives of Musset or Chopin, was shocked once by a case—treated by Balzac—of what she calls "a deception of the lips, the heart, and the senses". She concludes her letter to the novelist with the following words:

"The more I scrutinize my heart, my conscience and my religious beliefs, the more rigid I become in my views. Not only do I regard as a mortal sin—I use the word advisedly—sensuous deception in love, but I so regard even the illusion with which the senses try to deceive themselves in loves unworthy of the name.

"What I say, because I firmly believe it, is that unless one is in love with one's whole being, one should live, whatever may happen, in complete chastity."

This quotation, if paralleled with the life of its author, will well repay meditation.

CHAPTER XI

Action

Action is a beautiful word. The philosopher, the dramatist and the soldier know how to give it its full significance. Action is a translation of thought and might rank with artistic manifestations. It is really synonymous with life, as distinguished from mere vegetating, and is practically indiscernible from it, but, as I shall point out in a moment, many people mistake the appearances of it for the reality.

Action is the remedy for brooding, anxiety, concentration on self, hypertrophy of the Ego, exaggerated introspection and, in general, for the dangers attending an ill-guided interior life. It is the golden mean between Oriental annihilation and the obsessing search after pleasure of the hedonist. People who wistfully look towards the psychoanalyst, people who suffer from chronic hesitancy, who live in the hope of a universal formula applicable to all difficulties and plan endlessly before taking any step, diffident artists who never feel as if they had found themselves, should all plunge into action. There is no lack of such people in America, and probably the jargon of psychology is nowhere so familiar as it is in the United States. Yet, the American is essentially and proverbially active. His horror of wasted effort, his passion for self-realization, his aversion for contemplation not immediately leading to resolve, his sense of the practical and his respect for quantity all drive him into activity. So does his fear of all upsetting emotional states, especially when connected with unfamiliar intellectual causes, or his antipathy for speculative contradictions which to him mean either scepticism or a sustained cerebral effort to which he thinks himself unequal. From these he recoils into the gestures of his avocation, as poor Silas Marner shrank from the empty hole in his floor to his loom. Nowhere does the exclamation: do something! place the emphasis on *some* as sincerely as it does in America. Add the gregariousness and imitativeness so universal in the United States, the empirical tendencies imported from old England, and the innumerable chances which American opportunities and the American mobility give to the craving for action, and you will realize that the feverish passage from work to amusement and from amusement to practical discussions is almost a necessity for people living in America.

Only, all this means agitation more than action, and even when people have not been conscious of the difference, their own life gradually makes it clear to them. For we get tired of good times, and even success and luck will pall. With weariness and disgust ancestral puritanism returns, and the voice of conscience silences confused desires. And as the American is a thoroughly good fellow and seldom refuses to do one a good turn, his altruistic tendencies only need an opportunity to become conscious of themselves. Women, by fits and starts, go into social service. The men feel an increasingly definite craving to leave their imprint on something more permanent than a business or a fortune. Many, it is true, wait till their decline to make up their minds about how to satisfy this longing. Often it is not until they write their wills that the dread of losing a final chance leads them to decide in favor of this or that cause which somehow appeals to their imagination. Few rich men in America dare to die without leaving behind them a provision of this kind. But this procrastination is not universal. Many men, years before they die, are called to action by an interior illumination, by the *exposé* of some situation before which they find it impossible to remain passive, most often by some biography showing them what men and women in circumstances similar to their own have been able to do. No sooner have they had that revelation than their routine ceases to appeal to them, and mere money-getting, even the excitement of getting it, offers no gusto. Superior images take the place of those which, until then, had kept the soul-machine going. You see such people devoting all their energy to a school, a hospital, a museum or a collection, to the embellishment of their city, to philanthropy or to the diffusion of some idea which is expected to work in other people the same transformation of which the originator is conscious in himself. These people not only lead different lives but they become different persons, and the change can be noticed in their physiognomy. Experiences of this kind are recorded by the thousand in history or biography, and the consciousness of their existence, or mere allusions to their existence, are the vital fluid of spiritual life. Were it not for the *fascinatio nugacitatis,* the attraction of nothingness which the Biblical Wisdom books ridicule, or the superfluities which so-called civilization regards as necessities, men and women would not wait till disgust taught them fastidiousness before rising above trivial occupations and really beginning to live.

The remedy for waste, for the squandering of our most precious resources, lies primarily, of course, in substituting worth-while objects for valueless ones in our daily life. This change often seems spontaneous, although it may have been prepared by a long series of partial disappointments, but it is not, as a rule, the result of a purely mental choice. In most cases the lesson of life, a trial, a disappointment, a bereavement are active. Or some charm is at work. We meet a person whose way of looking at life seems superior and yet attractive. The sound of a voice, a mere smile passing judgment on a worldly remark, a dissenting silence in a chorus of triviality may be the revelation. Biographies or letters, sometimes a few talismanic verses have, many times, been the turning point in the life of a man so far unaware of anything nobler than his petty routine. So have acts of courage or examples of self-sacrifice. No human being would be at a loss to explain what is meant by the salt of the earth. Truth, beauty or nobility need only appear to subjugate.

From the moment a man is conscious of moral beauty he is also conscious of an attraction. His mind endlessly reverts to the object by which he is enchanted. He does not exactly test it, but by gazing at it in all sorts of environments, by building air-castles of all kinds in which to house it, he becomes familiar with all its possibilities. Happiness is inseparable from that enjoyment of an ideal, but the consciousness of a responsibility is also associated with elation. No man engrossed by a life-giving idea can be silent about it. It would have been preposterous for any except the transformed son of rich Bernardone to go round the Umbrian cities singing the praise of Poverty, but Francis of Assisi did it because he could not help doing it. The revelation of superhuman freedom belonging to perfect detachment from earthly possessions could not remain his own secret. He had to speak, as a happy child has to cry out, and no greater mistake can be made than to imagine him as obeying duty, unless it was the duty not to keep from others what intoxicated him with joy.

Forget Francis who was a saint, and because saintliness is not of daily occurrence may seem unreal. Think of that humble neighbor of yours who cannot be silent about some simple moral recipe he has discovered, or thinks he has discovered. Take away from him the something ordinary which perhaps makes him boresome, and you have an apostle. There are in this world of ours thousands who spend their lives disseminating some thought which they regard as illumination, justice, or joy. They all find a following. And when they become conscious that they have found that following and know that, even in their tiny circle, they are leaders, they become conscious of added dignity. With this consciousness another is born: the certainty that unless their life is above reproach their ideal will suffer the contempt which the contrast between a man's teaching and his example inevitably produces. No chief can afford to give the least impression of weakness or he will have the uncomfortable feeling that those who believe in him have to look away from his foibles. The immediate reward of noble action is that without any of the tactics recommended by moral technicians, it lifts up a man above himself.

There are other results. A man immersed in action has no time for trivialities in thought, speech or deed. The pained surprise visible on his face when they are forced upon him is not merely pathetic, it is eloquent. Many a time the torch has been passed from an apostle to an innocent intruder during an interview which, for the first time, revealed to idleness the virtues of pressure.

Action also increases mental resilience to a degree unsuspected till it is experienced. Newspaper men whose business it is to attend parliamentary debates are often surprised at the change noticeable in a politician's grasp of intricate questions the moment he becomes a Cabinet Minister, and has to do things instead of merely talking about them. Anybody who is subject to interviews also knows that his intellect is ten times more active when he is being professionally questioned than when he is merely conversing. The moment we feel responsible, especially when suffering people are looking up to us, or when what we say may decrease injustice or ignorance, we are conscious of a truly divine force in us which we had never suspected before.

Our moral strength is also benefited. Even selfishness, apparently frequent in leaders, becomes different from what it would be in a more trivial environment. Self-sacrifice is of daily occurrence. So, of course, is fearlessness. No man possessed of an idea to such a degree that he has to proclaim it cares for the consequences. History shows it on every page. What is not so well known, because it is invisible, is the fact that a man engaged in action, as well as a man engaged in vital intellectual considerations, ceases to fear death. The young artist who, in Daniel Chester French's group, sees Death opening the door of his studio, shows surprise and possibly indignation, but no fear. Fear never enters where there is a great ideal. Such are the virtues of action worthy of the name.

That it has its dangers is evident to anybody who has any experience of it or who has watched, often with some anxiety, noble men and women engaged in it. The chief danger is that, frequently, the means are mistaken for the end, or the joy of success crowds out the remembrance of one's ideals. It is better, in many cases, to fail or partially fail, than to succeed. For service always ennobles whereas success is perilously near mediocrity.

Often, too, the man working for a cause becomes too conscious of the human material on which he has to work and, instead of lifting it up to himself, descends to its level. Certain smiles, a beginning of toadyism, even in men and women of the first order, have left painful images in my memory. The solitary who wrote *The Imitation* was right in saying that you are less of a man every time you go among men. Using one's charm in order to persuade, instead of entirely relying upon truth, is detrimental to dignity and seems like a desecration.

However, these lowering influences can be counteracted. First and foremost by a constant recurrence to the contemplation of one's ideal. Comte, a positivist, advises giving two hours every day to such a contemplation and calls it prayer. All great men of action are incessantly meditating. Their ideal is such that all practical approaches to it seem far short of realization. No danger then of becoming vulgarized or complacent. The man who feels unworthy of serving a great cause blames all his failures on his own inadequacy.

Finally, the man of action, more than any other, needs a rule of life. He may be tempted to think that as he achieves results all the time he is winning for himself a right to more freedom than the contemplative can ever claim. This is partly true, and the necessities of a great cause should have the right of way. But, without a rule, the mind will indulge in vagabondage, success will assume undue proportions and the witnesses of this deterioration will wonder. Action requires the same unity of view, of purpose and of effort that the meditation of the philosopher demands.

CHAPTER XII

Expression

DEMOCRITUS says that expression is the shadow of action. It is not saying enough. Speech is an aspect of action and action seldom can dispense with it. Hence the importance, scarcely seen by most people, of what we say, and how and when and to whom we say it.

Indeed when we try to take cognizance of the virtue of language we find ourselves in the presence of such a wealth of complicated influences that our imagination is baffled. Clearly, since its first humble beginnings in the unseizable past, speech has developed in a surprising way, enriching itself as continuously and mysteriously as life, in its subtlest manifestations, may have done. Why do some languages seem to possess characteristic powers which do not exist in others? Why is Greek as intellectual as eighteenth century French and yet as soul-embracing as the English of Shakespeare? Is not Latin a voice, one of those low-pitched voices which cause everybody to turn around when certain women say even indifferent things? When Browning describes the Spanish name of a flower as "half-awakened song" he is not poetizing.

The same people do not say the same things when they speak English that they say when they speak

French. A good many years ago I spent a few weeks at a Cannes hotel where the Duke of Cambridge was also wintering. His dining-room was only separated from that of the friends I was visiting by a thin partition and every word said in one room could be overheard in the other. Sometimes the Duke's guests, in obedience to impalpable influences, would speak English, sometimes French. When they talked in English the staple of conversation chiefly consisted of facts relieved by anecdotes. The jolly old Duke would laugh loudly into his napkin. When French was preferred generalizations appeared, stale stories were replaced by witty and not too good-natured gossip, and the Duke would chuckle in a subdued guilty way.

On several occasions I have been conversing in English with American women who did not pretend they knew French. The tone of conversation was comradelike. The moment these ladies broke out into fluent French, the whole atmosphere was changed, and I knew my place as a mere man. Yet French women seldom act or even feel superior to males, but the language, with its inherited associations, gives them the aloofness they are not looking for. An American woman who would be as indifferent to conventionalities in French as she was in English, would lose caste.

Those things are only felt, but they are felt keenly, so keenly that the mysteriousness of the power of words ceases to intrigue us, though it is there all the same. Whenever we send syllables into the world their effect is as infallible on the people who hear them as it is on the ethereal waves. I may be giving a lecture on immortality. If I stop in the middle of it and just say: China, the astounded audience will, however, obey me; they will forget immortality and begin to visualize a vague geographical contour of China, with odd disconnected scenes imagined from the recent Chinese news. Again, you have just made a hundred dollars by a little extra job you had not counted upon. You tell the joyful story of your luck to a friend. He informs you that a similar job has brought him in a thousand dollars, whereupon your hundred ceases to exist as a source of happiness. A few words have destroyed it. We all know how the titles of books act. The same book which will only mildly interest you if it is entitled "Mythology" will become alluring if the title is changed to "Myths". Why? because words have an aura, and a rose by another name would not be exactly what we think a rose is. All that the Ancients have said about the bonds with which words chain our souls is true. Words are deeds. They, like writing, must have had at first something magical about them which they have never lost.

Therefore words ought to be used with care and with a proper sense of responsibility. The fundamental principle is the forgotten truism that we should only speak when we have something to say. Orientals who do it surprise us by their capacity for silence and by the eloquence of those silences. What we surmise of the conversation of the Ancients—through other evidence than the satire of their comic writers, or through purely literary devices like that employed by Cicero in his two monologues on *Divination*—leads us to the conclusion that they were not verbose. The brevity of a pointed answer to a question worth our while gives us an artistic pleasure.

But how rare it is! To most people talking is what reading has become: something apart from its object, a bodily, rather than a mental, exercise. Men accuse women of talking for talk's sake. But many men are incorrigible babblers. Who sits through the long day in the smoking-room of the train, talking, talking? Who says nothing, but says it through the hideous night in hotel-rooms or at the Club? I have been the victim of extraordinary performances. Men fight for the floor and keep it without compunction or even misgivings. In Europe something shameful still attaches to the words *bavard,* or chatter-box. I have never noticed the same nuance in America. A tattler is called a bore, but the definition of a bore as a fellow who talks about himself while you want to talk about yourself tells its own tale. It is understood and recognized that everybody has a right to talk about himself, so that the famous saying of Pascal about the hatefulness of the Ego is not translatable into English. People show the indulgence of complicity to men and women whose eager faces inform you, before you have said a word, that the moment they open their mouths it will be to treat you to insufferable details about their uninteresting lives.

It is bad enough to be victimized by an isolated bore when one is by oneself *sub cultro,* as Horace puts it, under the knife. But the ordeal is much worse when one is at his mercy in spite of the presence of seven or eight other people who should be a defence. This, I am sorry to say, happens especially in America, and if the art of conversation some day becomes a thing of the past in Europe as it is in the United States, American influences for once will really be responsible for the loss.

There is hardly a vestige of conversation left in America. Worse than that, the word has ceased to have any meaning. The question so familiar in Europe: "What was the subject of conversation at dinner last night?" is never heard in the United States, and if it were, it would sound as preposterous as might be the question: "What was the subject of conversation at your dance?"

Few indeed are the people who, hearing the word conversation, remember that the name, and, no doubt, the thing in its perfection, came from Italy. The guests at a house-party would sit in *circolo* to have a *conversazione,* that is to say, each one in his turn would give his opinion on some topic. Perhaps, before another generation has vanished, people will not know that a "general conversation" means one in which, no matter how many people are assembled, only one voice is heard at a time. Americans who always credit the "Latins" with vehemence and exuberance, would be surprised indeed to see how a dozen or even more people in Rome or Madrid, or Buenos Aires, can keep their native effervescence in check to enjoy a conversation. They have a sense of absolute freedom, yet they obey two rules which were impressed upon me in childhood till they became law: *pas d'apartés et pas de monologues;* no asides and no floor-holding! Asides especially were supposed to be the characteristic of a boor. This admixture of pleasure and profit, consciously yet not laboriously sought, is undoubtedly one of the most civilized enjoyments that urbanity has made possible for mankind.

"Why! that is the Club!" you exclaim, *"and nowhere is the Club more flourishing than it is in the United States!"*

Perfectly true. I have been admitted a few times to club deliberations, and I have retained a vivid memory of the capacity which American women show for knowing their minds and for expressing themselves lucidly, tersely and courteously. This shows that national habits are often inexplicable, for the same women, a moment after their deliberation was over, would take their part in a brain-racking chorus of multilogues which did not seem to inconvenience them in the least. American voices are accused of being shrill, although their natural quality ought to make them rather lower-pitched than the British falsetto, but how can anyone avoid shrillness in a bird-market? When there are six people in a room in the United States there are three conversations inevitably carried on in a high key, and dozens of times I have found that, even at a lunch party of four, it was impossible to suppress the rivalry of two voices. Reciprocal volleys are poured out as they used to be in the naval battles of yore when the guns answered one another nose to nose. Nothing is so laughable as a dinner-party of that kind given in honor of Mr. or Mrs. So-and-So. The poor lion has the look of having been caught in a pit-trap. Sometimes a lady next to him, straining her neck to hear what he says in the confusion, signals to the other guests that this distinguished person is saying something that it is unforgivable to miss, but they look at her blankly, or they wink and resume their piping or shouting. Presently they go home bragging about having met the famous novelist or astronomer, who, they add, "has not much to say."

What are the causes of this state of affairs which certainly did not exist in America sixty years ago, as many survivors still assert, not only in the more refined and secluded towns of New England, but even in places in the Middle West which possess a tradition? Why should Americans, who prove such excellent listeners at a lecture and love a serious discussion, show themselves such squanderers of words? Perhaps imported *nouveaux riches* who knew no better have started the odious revolution; sometimes an incongruous guffaw opens up a not altogether pleasing retrospect. Perhaps women, wanting to be amused and regarding a general topic as a rival, have compelled the man next to them to act as if they should be the centre of attention. I often find that after the men are left to themselves in the dining-room questions really worth while are started, and the guests find more pleasure in listening than in bawling. Almost certainly the chief cause is the habit which hostesses, for the opposed sakes of either magnificence or economy, have taken to give large parties instead of limiting themselves to the "number of the Muses". A general conversation is possible when eight or nine, not when twenty people, sit at dinner. It was not so when only one or two guests were added to the family dinner and found the father leading the conversation, as he still does in intelligent Jewish homes.

Many travelled American women resent the unjust inferiority which the hubbub habit gives to otherwise distinguished parties. One experience of real conversation is enough to show that no inveterate teller of stale stories dares to indulge his mania when seven or eight people staring at him in astonishment make him realize that stories are the stupid man's wit; no silly little egotist can retail her immature self to a whole circle. People who even once have felt how much the magnetism of a small but select audience can add to their powers, or who simply have had the revelation that conversation is an adventure the outcome of which never can be foreseen, crave the return of the experience. I often hear regrets and, once or twice, I have seen rebellion. If I had not witnessed the scene myself I could hardly believe that a State governor after vainly trying to put in a word which four ladies mercilessly drowned every time, lost his temper and struck the table with his fist, thundering that he "did not want to talk all the time but he wanted to talk some". When the ladies retired, leaving a trail of flying syllables behind them, he asked me if the women of my own country treated their men like that, and I told him a little story of Renan and Caro the philosopher which planted in him, I am afraid, an eternal longing.

Some hostesses are bold enough to start a reaction. "Do please, listen to this" is heard sometimes in a querulous tone. A friend of mine who is a rare appraiser of good things does all she can. When pandemonium becomes unbearable she clicks her glass, gracefully bows good-bye to the gentleman on her right and addresses herself to the gentleman on her left. Everybody else does the same, and there is a little lull of angry silence before the company start again with renewed vigor. The same lady, knowing that she is beaten and being the kind who never acknowledges herself beaten, sometimes, when the dessert comes, institutes a sort of forum which it takes a few minutes to realize is only a conversation. It is a success every time. One feels then how many excellent things must have perished in the storm of voices still raging a minute before, and how much a campaign for conversation-dinners or a League of the Solo Voice would do for a country which to-day has no conversation but which, however, possesses all that could make first-rate conversation.

It is too evident that there can be no action through words when words are crazily let loose. What happens is that the effusiveness and the lack of self-control created in such an atmosphere finally bring a sensation of barrenness as if the tired soul had been parched up for ever. Action must be premeditated, guided and sustained. If we want our life not to be aimless, if we hate to think of our words as still-born seeds, we must never approach company without being on our guard against its sterilizing influence. Not everybody would endorse what Keats said about a room full of people—not only grown-ups, but children—distressing and exhausting his soul. But it is less because we do not feel as Keats did than because, being indifferent to the loss of our personality, we do not feel the dangers threatening it as he did. Most men are, or have been, conscious of the nervousness caused by the presence of their fellow-men. Some know they are not at all themselves when women are present, while practically everybody has a vague consciousness that company expects from them not their best but their most trivial, and are tempted accordingly.

Simple remedies will be found to work. Stop at the door of the house you are going to enter and stay there motionless during a minute or two. Or, as I said before, slacken up your pace to a crawl as you draw near it. Or repeat slowly and with long pauses one of those poems which we all regard as a sort of talisman, as if it belonged to us and to nobody else. When the blood ceases to tingle in your arteries or sing its odd song in your ear, remember the something in your innermost to which you may not be actually devoting, but to which you would like to devote, your whole life, whether it be truth, beauty, or moral rarity. This you will not do without a consciousness of personal dignity and an accompanying resolve not to give in and not to give up. A sense of responsibility will not be far and you will not shrink from it. Perhaps you will then remember one of the few conversations really worth while you once had with some fellow-being. Ten minutes in the twilight with a person whom you felt really possessed of an idea, and of a passionate longing to make you believe in it, may still be alive in your memory as they are in mine.

That is the kind of atmosphere in which thought-transference, or the magic of desire, are sure to work. Many times we have felt its irresistibility. I have seen a lover of animals create it in a second when expostulating with cruel but instantly subdued people. I have felt it only yesterday when an old lady started moralizing about an "unseen force" which had always helped her. Every word she said hit the mark like an infallible arrow. We too can say such things and produce the same effect. If it is not to-day it will be to-morrow, or it may be in ten years. I laughed, as a child, when I was told of a Hindoo sage who had the road swept in front of him lest, inadvertently, he should destroy the life crawling there. But I never see the quick-legged caterpillar going about his business across the garden-walk without remembering that long-dead Buddhist priest.

Indeed words can be actions, and, when they are not, they are a waste for him who says them and more or less of an insult for him who has to hear them. As Disraeli said, life is too short for us not to try to make it great.

CONCLUSION OF THIS SECTION

Two things are of paramount influence in any life that would raise itself above the petty routine which most people call living: the first is the vision of the kind of ideal for which each one of us is naturally predisposed; the second is devotion to that ideal.

For, the Ideal in its own nature is magnetic, that is to say irresistible and, like love, it makes everything easy, while devotion is synonymous with self-denial and embellishes a man's soul as it ennobles his physiognomy. There is no danger of exaggerated asceticism in a life devoted to a cause. Nor is it to be feared that the blemishes habitual to unaided human nature will survive in the flame lighted by a great thought or a great desire.

No man or woman who has had the revelation of what the higher life means has ever resisted the desire to spread that revelation. And, while doing so, they have never been able to tolerate in themselves littlenesses which would bring into discredit or ridicule the cause for which they are working. Beauty, devotion and moral perfection are inseparable. As for the methods in their service they are secondary.

B. THE SPIRITUAL PLANE

Introductory Note

The state of consciousness constantly alluded to in the previous chapters is a happy tension, an aspiration, natural and effortless, towards a life made not only beautiful but fascinating by noble thoughts, sentiments or actions. This fascination is accompanied by an aversion for trivialities and by an indifference to self which recall the behavior of an artist entranced by the magic of the sky. The vision outshines everything else.

What does this mean if not that men and women who lead a beautiful life are under the influence of something exterior to themselves, leading them on by its own attraction? They may, for a long time, be only vaguely aware of this haunting presence, but some day they inevitably bow to it. They cannot escape the realization that they are part of a vast spiritual concert in which thousands of like-minded people give themselves up to the attraction of the universal good. The concert began long before they joined in it, and it will go on long after they have apparently ceased to be in it. This they hardly mind, for they see how little they contribute to the harmony. But the humble acknowledgment of this inadequacy is accompanied by the certainty that *something permanent* must exist endlessly to go on with the divine drama which ravishes them.

What is that permanent something? Nothing else than the Spirit without whom there would be neither Truth, nor Beauty, nor magnetic Ideal in the universe. This Spirit may be called by a score of names;

some people may always refuse to call it God; they may even feel reluctant to word a full assent to its existence. But, for all that, its existence will be the support and the *raison d'être* of their own.

What does this mean? That after Science has led us on to philosophy, philosophy in its turn, can lead us higher up to the spiritual plane. This is what has happened to Plato and even more strikingly to his famous disciples, Plotinus, Iamblichus or Porphyry. Do not be shy of long-dead Greek philosophers using a discouraging vocabulary. If you will only look up those great men in the *Encyclopaedia* you will never forget your hour with them. You will find that the soul-ascent they have all experienced is something intelligible, natural and enchanting. Gradually you will regard what has happened to them—indeed what has happened to you through your reading about them—as a revelation of infinite value.

Why is it, then, that if we substitute the word "religious" for "spiritual" we shrink? Why is the word "religion" even more formidable than its adjective? And why do we hesitate, almost in terror, before changing the name of the Spirit to God?

CHAPTER I

What Religion Is Not

In his popular book entitled *Orpheus,* M. Salomon Reinach defines religion as "the sum of the superstitious beliefs which hinder the legitimate working of man's faculties." Many people who will think this definition, to say the least of it, unsympathetic are, however, convinced in their hearts that religion is a constraint. Hence the lurking aversion, the reverence gone sour, which so many of our contemporaries are conscious of when the very word religion is mentioned in their hearing. Other words like law, morals, or duty may awaken a similar repulsion but not in the same degree. The reason is that they are less definite and seem to limit human activity within a more circumscribed field, whereas religion is regarded as a tyrant both of the intellect and of life.

People seldom take the trouble to check off, with a view to organizing, their opinions, and so the impression I speak of may remain inarticulate, but it is there all the same. What can be more frequent than the general statement that religion clashes with modern ideas? Religion is supposed to force upon us a history of the world, of creation, of man, of his development and of his so-called relations with the

Godhead which at present sounds so childish that no refutation of it is necessary. People take it for granted that this view of religion has had its day. A far from anti-religious woman lately said in my hearing that Sunday-school either must forget its Fundamentalist astronomy, geology, and pre-history or its attendance must dwindle to nothing. Other people, sufficiently well-informed to have heard of what Mr. Santayana calls the "Christian epic" but is wrongly, though frequently, referred to as the "Christian myth", defy believers to give the traditional sequence of the Christian facts—from the Fall in Eden to the Redemption—in quotations from the Bible or the creeds. "Not only our ears would rebel", they add, "but your own tongue would be paralyzed." Their conclusion is that it is with this epic as with all legendary tales: they survive as long as they can bear the test of oral transmission; the moment they sound as an echo of the past a shadow of them may subsist in people's sentiments or attitudes, but they can never again command credence as they used to do. Another conclusion, which many seem anxious to emphasize, is that when people, even of the same denomination, are challenged to state what are the articles of their creed, they are seen to differ in an astonishing degree, the most intelligent striving to reduce dogma to a minimum.

According to the same critics, supported by millions who having only emotions cannot lay any claim to being called critics, our moral independence, our right to live as our nature dictates, is, even more than our intellectual freedom, threatened by religion.

What people eat and how much of it they should eat, their sexual relations, their right to pre-marital experiences, their right to divorce, their right to determine for themselves the number of their children, are interfered with by the churches, and even by the State wherever the two powers have not been separated. To modern men and women this surveillance of their actions seems unbearable. The tone of rebellious triumph which they assume in scoffing at it shows that, on no point, are they as sensitive as they are about this. Yet, they have other complaints. They abuse religion as a kill-joy, as the inventor of a notion, sin, which introduces bitterness where otherwise only joy would be, as the advocate of penitence or sacrifice where the delight of action could be accompanied by positive results instead of merely leading to annihilation. Above all they think the preaching of hell blasphemous as well as immoral, and point out in triumph that many so-called orthodox parents have made their aversion for it so clear to their own clergy that a sermon on hell will soon offer only an historic interest.

It is useless to point out that this general view of religion as constraint is popular: it fills the press in the most unexpected quarters, it is taken for granted in fiction and the drama, and it is discussed from the lecture-platform by crusaders who do not, for one moment, suspect that it may be worse than superficial.

Yet, a little effort to analyze and criticize, would suffice to show how restricted such a view of religion is.

How can thinking people imagine that science and religion have the least contact at any point? What is there in common between the consciousness of spiritual realities and such questions as the age and constitution of matter, the apparition of life in the world, the date and manner of man's apparition on earth? Only intellectual rashness can account for such a confusion of issues.

"Yet, has not religion exhibited many instances of that very rashness you complain of? Has not the Church condemned Galileo for a scientific opinion?"

"Which are you accusing, religion or the Church, that is to say Churchmen? Are you sure of your vocabulary?"

"I mean Churchmen, the authorities in the Church."

"And I notice that your tone, instead of being more triumphant and indignant, drops to a matter-of-fact medium. This is strange, for the reverse ought to happen. You ought to be more contemptuous of mere men than of a craving in our nature which every great philosopher treats with reverence, often with loving respect."

"I am only speaking as everybody does."

"But that is exactly what you should not do. If you repeat what everybody says you will never think. Churchmen may make, they do make, all sorts of mistakes in their interpretations of their own creed, but how does that affect religion? It is in reality the strongest proof that religion and science can never come in contact. Are there any Churchmen left to-day who say, or even think, that the sun revolves round the earth?"

"Of course not."

"Of course not. Observe, it is not because the doctrine of Copernicus is more solidly established at present than it was when it was propounded. Less than thirty years ago, Henri Poincaré, a great mathematician, anticipating relativity, raised no contradiction when he wrote that we have as much reason to say that the sun revolves around the earth as to maintain the contrary proposition."

"Why is it then?"

"Because Churchmen do not care. They know that scientific questions are no concern of theirs."

"Why did they not realize it before?"

"Because progress is slow and genius rare. You and I are using language which we do not suspect will sound strange and remote to our descendants. One man, however, at the time of Galileo's condemnation, did say a few words which put the whole question in a nutshell and antedated all that has been said about it since. *'The Bible'*, cardinal Robert Bellarmine said, *'tells us how to go to heaven, but not how the heavens go.'* "

"I never heard that. I always associate Bellarmine with German beer-mugs. But why was Bellarmine the only one?"

"Because, as I was telling you, plain commonsense is as rare as genius. So-called orthodox views of scientific questions are, in most cases, not religious at all. They are the popular scientific view of the day, nothing else. After a generation or two this view becomes slowly modified. By that time it is seldom alluded to; it is 'up attic', as they say in Vermont. In less than a hundred years after that, people have moved into new houses and the junk has been left behind, forgotten as if it had never existed. I know you would love meeting a Fundamentalist punch-bag who would irritate you by defending geocentrism. But you will not find him, even in Tennessee. Wait a hundred years and what still irritates you to-day will be 'up attic' with all the rest. It is at the garret-door already."

"*What then* is *religion?*"

"Wait a moment. For the time being a tremendous step onward will have been taken if you are convinced, to your satisfaction and not to your disappointment, that religion is not science, and that, even in questions concerning, for instance, its own history historians should preferably be heard. Did not Max Müller know more about the history of Indianism than dozens of Hindoo communities put together?"

Religion is not an unreasonable constraint on our life any more than it is a constraint on our reason. The contention of this book is that our moral ideal appeals to us more through its beauty than because of its other aspect as duty. Another certainty underlying these pages is that every man possessed of an ideal which engrosses his whole being, is inevitably and continuously inclined to link its presence in his soul with the presence of the Spirit in the world. There is no more constraint in this than in a flower's tendency to follow the course of the sun. Yet, even morals, properly analyzed, will be found to differ from religion. Much more so the minor morals on which childish hostility to religion often fastens its dislikes. Much more so mere usages found in all institutional religions but which have little or nothing to do with the essence of religion. See how religions vary in their dealing with marriage. Have Ramadans anything more specifically religious than hygienic in them? People who imagine they have show no more logic than the man who, discovering that the Archbishop of Toledo, like everybody else in Spain, eats meat on Fridays, thinks himself entitled to polygamy. As a conclusion let it be said that the millions of people, young and old, who clamor to-day that, if they were religious, their life would be interfered with have no idea of what religion is.

How are we to account for this astounding misunderstanding of an all-important issue? Can we not add a little psychology to what was said on the subject in Part One?

First of all, we should look for the cause in the usual sources of human errors, viz., lack of information or faulty logic. I have noted elsewhere that ninety-five people in a hundred imagine that, because they *wonder* about an issue, they are considering it. Curiosity certainly is the root of knowledge, but mere wondering cannot be compared with thought or research. Observe people's faces at a debate on religion. A certain eagerness will denote the usual interest in a fight accompanied by the very proper desire that narrow-mindedness should be exposed and routed. Occasional glimpses of thoughtfulness will reveal that, with most of the audience, a lurking hope still prevails that what they vaguely think of as *their* religion may be preserved. But at no moment will you notice the alertness which means that people could be the principals in such a duel instead of passively witnessing it. People do not think about big issues. All the time you hear them alluding to religion, morals, the principles of politics, love, death, beauty. Ask them how many hours, how many minutes they have devoted to a real examination of those questions, their smile will be an almost touching confession. Ignorance, inertness, are the rule.

Anybody who has had to do with theologians well read enough and independent enough to be above the mere retailing of text-books must have been impressed by a tendency they constantly show to discard what is not essential. Often they startle by unexpected utterances. One of them, a perfectly orthodox teacher, once gave currency to the adage: "Sacraments are for men, not men for sacraments." Ponder this saying, place it in its real perspective, imagine the mass of prejudice through which it had to work its way, and you will see how much intellectual boldness went into its terse wording. I once heard the saintly bishop Martin de Gibergues say: "One can be baptized without water, be purified of one's sins without a priest, and receive communion without a host". Nothing but pure orthodox theology in this, to be sure, yet what a revelation, often what a shock to literal people expecting nothing but literalness! Let anybody follow the spiritual trend in the teaching of the most enlightened students of Christianity, from Origen to Newman, and he will see how often the trees must have hidden the forest from him, how formidable the confusion of the essential with the inconsequential is in most minds. But it will be so as long as men imagine they can learn without studying, or have a right to speak without having thought.

However, the chief cause of the almost world-wide misunderstanding of religion is to be found in a deeper stratum than any so far referred to: it is nothing less than the almost equally universal misunderstanding concerning God Himself. Something has been said in Part One to account for that misconception, but it is so basic an error, its consequences are so far-reaching that a full investigation of it cannot be superfluous.

CHAPTER II

What God Is Not

God, the Supreme Being, the source of all reason and goodness, is not, cannot be, what millions of people object to when they think of religion. For there is about the name of God, as it strikes the ears of many men, a coldness, a remoteness, which, in spite of ourselves, reacts on our own conception of the Deity.

Hardly any child grows up without hearing God mentioned in a variety of circumstances until it is inevitable that a vague but comprehensive notion should correspond to the name. But how crude and erroneous that notion is! Perhaps through the unwisdom of preachers quoting metaphysicians before an unprepared audience, God appears as self-sufficient and supremely happy; but from the very fact that He is independent for His happiness from anything that is not within Himself, especially from the fact that not one of the words here used escapes the danger of misapprehension, He also appears as selfishly happy. He is supposed to be indifferent to us, indifferent to our happiness or unhappiness. Worse than that, He seems deliberately to prepare the wretched lot of his unfortunate creatures. We speak of the "jealous gods" and we touch wood, or go through some other little rite as childishly primitive, but while we say "gods" we really mean God. Our "God" is envious, irritable and treacherous. When we substitute, as we often do, the calvinistic for the Hebrew vocabulary, we make matters even worse. God purposely creates us weak so that we may be tempted beyond our powers; He brings us out of nothingness in order to damn us. How many young children, catching their first glimpse of such a God, have felt their souls full of terror which has bred rebellion! What most of them in their evil moments say to their parents: "I never wanted to be born!" they have also thought in passionate helplessness of the ultimate source of life itself. Anybody with some knowledge of human nature will admit the truth of this description.

Is it to be wondered at therefore that, in their hearts, many men are so afraid of this "God" that, as Marcion felt in the second century, they would rather have Him non-existent, and they pray for logical arguments strong enough to rid them of His unbearable presence? And does not this mean that, as Marcion also felt, they, in a deeper region of their consciousness, cherish a certainty that the arguments must exist somewhere, invincible, and that between the real God and themselves there is only a witch's veil of cruel illusions? The strange thing is that, close by them, jostled by them every day, live millions of men and women whose faces radiate a different conception; not far from them mystics are lifted up to a superhuman level by continuous commune with the Spirit, while classical writings like those of Emerson could show them, half way between mysticism and philosophy, a state of mind approximating the peak of human happiness entirely due to a purified conception of the Supreme Being. How can we account for the existence, side by side, of a notion of God meaning help and happiness, with another meaning misery in the heart and blasphemy in the mind?

One of the most obvious causes is that while philosophy was rising to its life-giving conceptions it has made them unintelligible by clothing them in metaphysical formulas. It should have been the business of the preacher to translate these into the popular language, but the preacher has been unequal to the effort, and finding ready at hand in his daily liturgy the crude epithets which Israel applied to Iahve, he has used them without being able, as the Biblical writers were, to glorify them by poetry. Hence the survival of a God, jealous, irritable and revengeful. As a matter of fact, while the progress of science and philosophy was compelling mankind to crystallize its noblest intellectual effort round the divine name, the popular notion of God has remained corrupted by accretions going back, some of them, to the cave-man, so that average minds may see God written with an ennobling capital but what they actually read is only god.

Even Christians, whom the Gospel has helped to rise high above the concepts of the Old Testament, will be found in their habitual thoughts to give little or no attention to the Father or to the Trinity and, properly analyzed, this indifference will be found to hark back to the propensities of the early Greek converts much more than to dogmatic definitions generally ignored. The almost complete oblivion in which the Holy Spirit—in spite of constant references made to Him in the New Testament and in the liturgy—is held by the majority of Christians is traceable to the same intellectual habits.

In other words, the popular notion of God is still that of a Superman. The progress of astronomical knowledge, and its popularization during the past four centuries, may have so enlarged the Superman-God that human imagination has been compelled to drop the usual attributes of man as it strove to follow the deity to the almost unthinkable limits of the universe, but the original misconception survives. This helps us to understand how it is possible that the problem of God should still be inseparable in most minds from the problem of evil. As long as Ahriman survived with his nefarious power it was relatively easy to visualize Ormuzd as the source of all light and all purity. Now Ahriman has disappeared and the feeble intelligence of mankind, not knowing what to do with evil, lazily lays the burden of it on its God without being conscious of either blasphemy or destructive contradiction. The god whom millions dread and are not far from abhorring is not God.

CHAPTER III

A Higher Notion of God

Over against the crude idea of the Supreme Being discussed in the previous chapter is another to which our increasing knowledge of the Universe obviously points. Revert once more—you never can do it too often—to the broadest and most visible lineaments of the evolution of the world. You see inorganic matter passing into living substances similar to it in their constituents, but entirely different in their behavior; in time these organic bodies, instead of being, like the sponge, irresponsive to what is going on around them, will show reactions to heat or cold or pressure; later on again this reaction will undergo a transformation of so marvellous a character that a lifetime cannot exhaust the wonder of it; it will become vision, matter will *see,* that is to say, will seize what is outside it; later on again, this vision, after untold eons of passivity, will become active: it will range curiously over what is within its reach. Simultaneously a sort of inward vision, consciousness, will have made its appearance; reflection will be born and an entirely new picture will be produced. Instead of just existing, the world will be *thought,* an astounding process, and, being thought, it will be organized, the newly-born intellect striving to distinguish, in its phenomena, between what is a cause and what is an effect. Finally this curiosity will develop into something even higher: evaluation will be introduced, the capacity for distinguishing between plus and minus in a domain which will be called the moral one; this is not all, the human intellect, assisted by a tendency deeper than mere comprehension, will strain towards the betterment of the universe; it will associate its power with that of the mysterious something at work under it all, and the word sanctity will have a meaning.

Who can visualize this development—which is a scientific certainty if there is to be certainty anywhere—and resist the conclusion that, under matter, must be something superior which our languages, doing the best they can, call Spirit? The Monist or Materialist succeeds in doing it, but at what cost? He first endows matter with the attributes of God and then declares that electric waves, or sheets, with sufficient time and chances, will ultimately develop into the mind of Plato, or even the soul of Christ. But, first of all, he has to beg the whole question and renounce, about this one issue, all the logic habitual to him. Is it surprising that there should be in his average type something so awkwardly ordinary and stubbornly narrow? No amount of asseverations or denials will avail: take away the spiritual explanation and not only the universe will lose all intelligibility, but the highest tendencies in our nature will become insoluble puzzles.

Most people's clocks are slow. Because the echoes of the battle fought by culture, since the Renaissance, against an inferior notion of God are still in our ears, many men imagine themselves to be in the vanguard of free thought when they resist the spiritual explanation. But the least acquaintance with the theories and tendencies of all the great scientists to-day would show them how uninformed they are. As for the philosophers, those at all events who have counted in the history of thought, they never varied. The whole long list of them is eloquent. Who would compare Cabanis or d'Holbach to Kant? And how dwarfed and isolated Haeckel seems to-day in his narrow system! Besides, take up any of the general re-examinations of values recently published in Europe or America, you will invariably notice this: even when the writers are the most resolutely hostile to institutional religions or to the classical basis of morals you see them gradually veering to a religious attitude. No sooner are they through with the analytical—and generally destructive—part of their work, than the craving which impels them to write makes them strive towards something constructive. They had come to curse—or to be fair to them, let us say that they had been led to curse—now they cannot resist their longing to have something to bless. You see them with their faces to the East, anxiously awaiting the dawn. And have you noticed that people who insist that they can build up a religion without a God strongly object at the same time to being called Atheists? A far cry this, from the eighteenth century. It shows that, if there is only too rife a tendency to point out the weak parts of theological systems, there is, in brilliant individuals, as well as in the crowds they lead, a keen desire to see the essentials of Theism preserved. Go over history and you will find, at every epoch, traces of these two tendencies, and perhaps you will understand that, instead of opposing each other, they are complementary.

But who, or what, is that spiritual agency without which the world and our mind would be chaos, without which neither truth, nor beauty, nor goodness would have a meaning? Is it more than a concept which our logic compels us to receive, but which corresponds to no being endowed with personality?

What God is no philosopher has ever been able to say, because philosophy has to express itself in words, and words, only feebly expressing even concrete realities, can never be an adequate representation of spiritual ones. There can be no hope of the finite grasping the infinite, of the accidental coping with the necessary, or of the imperfect measuring up to the perfect. These are evident impossibilities. The first stage towards full comprehension of the divinity ought to be a clear view of all the data in the problem of the universe, and we know only too well how far we are, and shall always be, from such a view. Hence the fundamental inadequacy of even the most stupendous genius to the comprehension of what God is. When Pascal, an impassioned believer, tells us that about God we never can tell "if He is or what He is", there is no other meaning to his words. There is nothing else either in the well-known criticism of the proofs of the existence of God made by Kant, who however regarded that existence as a postulate. Similar expressions, by the score, to be found in the philosophers endlessly refer to the impossibility for beings imprisoned in a narrow cell at the core of the universe to know what its circumference is like. So, we have to be satisfied with the terms least likely to lead us astray. Are there any?

It seems unquestionable that, in spite of its sanctity, in spite of the innumerable references made to it by great poets and great thinkers, the word God, as a human term, is not satisfactory. It has too long a past; it is too charged with conflicting associations; it has been used in too many different perspectives both by ecclesiasticism and by people violently opposed to ecclesiasticism; what is worse, it has been blasphemed too often for it not to show a fringe in which theism, paganism, and pure unbelief mix up their colors. Sometimes sensitive souls perceive something frigid in it: it is only the cold residuum of age-long controversies.

It has seemed many times that the word Spirit, familiar equally to the thinker, the poet and the believer—since, as I said, it fills the books of the New Testament—must be free from those disadvantages. That name has never been and can never be blasphemed, it only awakens helpful associations, and its very etymology, (breath or breeze) humble though it may be, connects it with the first efforts at philosophy made by primitive mankind. Indeed it is difficult for a reflective mind not to retranslate the word God into the word Spirit whenever an effort at accuracy appears to be required. It would seem, therefore, as if this word should be more familiar than it is, and the present writer will never be grateful enough to the Catechism, learned in childhood, which defined God as "a Spirit, endowed with eternity, infinity and perfection" as well as

...h the creative power. The danger of falling into anthropomorphism, or of seeing God as a Superman, is reduced to a minimum the moment the Supreme Being is referred to by a spiritual term. Who does not see how much mankind owes to Christ for the simple substitution of Father for Iahve or Adonaï? The restrictions which inherited ignorance or narrowness attaches to the name of God are dropped with the sound of that name.

However it would not be enough to have found a proper name for the essential Good without which the Universe would only be matter. The way to God is partly intellectual, but it is something else. If we want that intelligence of the divine which will not only illuminate but impregnate us, we must not only recognize the Spirit but also live in constant communion with Him.

CHAPTER IV

What Religion Is

RELIGION etymologically means a bond or a connection. It is in fact a bridge between the visible and the invisible and should primarily be regarded as the key to a riddle, the explanation of a mystery. The mystery—without the revelation of the Spirit—lies in the world about us as well as in the presence of unaccountable aspirations in our consciousness. Let it become clear that there is something beyond matter, and at once a sense of intelligibility will have been substituted for darkness.

As everybody knows, the sacred books of India are called the *Vedas,* a word evidently connected with Greek or Latin roots referring to vision or direct knowledge. Religion to the Hindoo is the removal of a veil.

That is what it should be to everybody. The inclusion into it of a moral discipline, or especially of ritual usages, is obviously secondary, and the sullen semi-surrender to religion which is so frequent in Latin countries is an absurdity. To include unwelcome compulsion in the notion of religion can only be the result of inherited misapprehension.

If we want to understand the true nature of religion we must endeavor to re-create for ourselves the atmosphere prevalent in the Eastern Mediterranean countries during the periods immediately preceding or following the birth of Christ. Innumerable engraved stones bear a word which explains the aspirations of the cultivated world at that time as well as its religiousness. *Soteria*, salvation, is that word. People wanted that grand vague thing, salvation, and felt sure it must come to them through a rite, but a rite consecrating the whispered revelation of a secret.

A scene which we only imagine must have actually taken place many times in the Greek cities of the Asiatic coast: A guest is seated at the supper-table. His hosts are intelligent questioning people, eager for *Soteria,* and who may perhaps have looked for it in some one of the mystery-religions from farther East. A fish has been served, and the Ephesian guest is gazing at it thoughtfully, every now and then also looking at his friends with an admixture of eagerness and uncertainty. He is a recent convert to Christianity, and the strange capacity of the letters making up the Greek word *ichthus,* a fish, to mean "Jesus-Christ, son of God, Savior" is still a joy to him. His hosts notice his look, easily draw him out, and he tells them the secret: believe that Jesus was the son of God; rise to a higher moral level than that you have hitherto known; and live ever after in *agallasis,* or joyful bliss. The whole of *Soteria* lies in this simple revelation.

It was never difficult for Greeks to believe that such a personage as Jesus of Nazareth was the son of God, and, in many instances, the revelation was no sooner made than it was welcomed, while *agallasis* was a matter of course.

That is the spirit in which religion should be received. Reluctance in accepting it is absurdity as much as blasphemy, and becomes unintelligible the moment the meaning of the word has been made clear. Without religion the world is a torturing puzzle; with the knowledge of the Spirit the joy of its comprehension fills the soul.

However, there is another aspect of the religious attitude, the absence of which is inconceivable if religion is properly understood. That is the natural striving of the soul, now sure of the existence and omnipresence of the Spirit, to achieve union with Him. All thinkers who are not mere intellectualists and all poets who are not pure emotionalists feel that inclination so strongly that they cannot resist it. To them the word God sums up all that they regard as attractive and magnetic; therefore they are not conscious of any sacrifice in obeying the attraction. Religion is as natural as the love of beauty.

The literature describing the ascent of the soul towards God and the results of the desire for mystical union fills libraries. India, Egypt and Persia had their mystics as well as Israel. Plato and the Platonists, Plotinus, Porphyry, Proclus, all passionately tended to a union with God which Porphyry calls ecstasy, but which is only access to the Spirit through growing indifference to matter. The Greek and Oriental mysteries had no other object than to bring the soul into immediate communication with the Deity. The many illuminists who, from Swedenborg to Victor Hugo, have described their journey in quest of the divine all place the assent of the whole soul ahead of a mere intellectual process. As for the Christian mystics, whose experience has been recorded for us in the minutest detail, they all rise to ecstasy,—the object of their common initiator, the Platonist Dionysius—and they all would agree with the author of the *Imitation* that it is better to experience than to define it.

The principle of mysticism is similar to that short cut to intellection which we call the intuitive process. When Socrates felt the presence and guidance of his *daimon* he gave no thought to the dialectics for which he is famous. The many Ancients who expected illumination from the incoherent speeches of madness, or from dreams or presentiments, evidently shared the same belief in an intellectual process quicker than ratiocination. Both intuition and mysticism prefer direct contact to inference. This is accomplished, first of all, by not wasting time on fruitless intellectual argument. The *Imitation* recommends "belief first and understanding afterwards", and these words, like all similar pronouncements, often revolt the mind. However, the same words are quoted with approval by no other person than the positivist and ultra-intellectualist, Auguste Comte. The reason is that, in matters involving the whole soul and not merely its intellectual surface, understanding is the result of experience much more than of a logical process, and Comte, as well as his disciple Herbert Spencer, had soul enough to be sure of that. But how can that be done? What should a willing person, with just the spiritual belief as a foundation, do in order to come in direct contact with the Spirit?

The process has been described hundreds of times by the mystics.

First of all leave out as much of yourself as can

be left out, and disentangle yourself from matter, that is to say, from that which is fundamentally inconsequential and gives the appearance of pleasure rather than the reality of happiness. Then retreat into yourself, into your very innermost, till you are face to face with your own soul. Let even your soul be silent, *sileat et ipsa anima,* till it will be conscious of complete interior solitude. At that stage you will find it impossible not to remember the omnipresence of God, and the presence of the Spirit in your spirit. Inevitably, you will be conscious of a humble longing, a prayerful hope, accompanied by the certainty that even if you never reach ecstasy this effort of your soul will have been its own reward. Such is the religious act.

"But what about prayer? Is not prayer the fundamental religious act?"

"Prayer is what has just been described: it is adoration, or recognition, and it is longing and union."

"But is not prayer, as usually understood, chiefly petition?"

It cannot be denied that, in all religions, this aspect of prayer is visible and often emphasized. The Church has her litany which is one long petition, and the prayers of the Christian liturgy, like the prayers of Israel, are for peace and sufficiency. Some superior minds will make fun of the poor Italian mother who prays the measles away. They call that superstition, and it may even be idolatry, but there is no superstition where a sense of human inadequacy, helped by a vivid consciousness of the cruelty of life is felt. Prayer is longing plus a sense of impotence. The longing may stay on the inferior level where the measles are prayed away, or rain is prayed for, but it would be rash to infer that it is always so. A mother returns from church where her children have been in her mind as they always are, yet you can read on her face something different from what was there before she went. Clearly, during that visit to church, the level of the poor soul has gone up one or several degrees: it has risen to prayer. How? The woman has wished perhaps her weakness to be strengthened, perhaps her deficiencies to be less painful. It is enough: the real attraction of the Spirit has been felt, and the first stage of union has been entered on.

For, prayer, in its essence, cannot be distinguished from union, and Tennyson defines it well as:

that mystery
Where God-in-man is one with man-in-God.

In the glow of that union everything else ceases to be visible. When a poor artist, with all his might, wishes for another visitation from that fitful thing which he calls genius, he forgets the sordidness of the cramped atelier, the insufficient food and clothing, the anxiety and uncertainty of the morrow. For he knows well (read Gauguin's letters) that clothes, food and lodging count for nothing as long as inspiration is there. So with the mystic who has known, were it only for one instant, the presence of God. How could he pray for anything beside that? He cannot misinterpret religion and prayer: his experience tells him that they are the supreme joy possible to man.

There is a saying of Mahomet's which sounds too

Oriental not to surprise our Western ears, but which however expresses the deep truth: "Above all things I like perfumes, and above all things I like women, but I like prayer even more." The man who wrote this knew what is meant by the repose of the soul in God.

"But how rare this, in its proper degree, must be!" you say, *"how inaccessible!"*

Certainly some people have more talent for religion than others, and unbelievers who stubbornly repeat: persuade me, convince me! do not know how comical they are. Mystics are as rare as artists. But if only a few can hear or obey the supreme call, it can be understood and revered by everybody. That is enough. Why should we not, within even restricted possibilities, endeavor to answer it? When we shabbily pray, for instance, that Bolshevism may stay where it is and not come too near our bank deposits, we can be a little less inferior if we admit and deplore that we are inferior. Our true self speaks through our desires or regrets.

A third aspect of the religious state of consciousness could be called collaboration with God. What the Spirit is doing in the world is to lift it up to the level of truth, beauty or goodness. Whoever obeys a desire to make his surroundings nobler or more beautiful, whoever works for a cause, even if he only gives a kind word and a smile to the children who buy trifles from him, is working with the Spirit.

When this collaboration with God reaches a certain degree of consciousness, it produces two results. In the first place it makes moral transformation a necessity. Nobody can exhort his neighbor, or even wish his neighbor, to live on the higher level without living on it himself. He may feel that he is thereby gaining beauty as well as personal magnetism. If he is more conscious of these additions to his power than convinced of their necessity he will be putting gold dust in his crucible before trying to transmute his lead, and all the transmutation will be a sham. But in most cases he will feel that sincerity is the condition of improvement.

The other necessary element in collaborating with God is the union with Him described above. You may devote your every effort to a crusade, if the crusade becomes an end in itself the crusader will lose. That is why there are in the United States so many good people and so few saints. The attraction of action in itself, the delight of doing something, anything, is too strong for most people. But the results are not always good. The Bible goes deeper than it seems to do when it says that the Lord dwelleth not in turmoil. This means that whoever is engaged in raising the level of thought or action in the world can only do so effectively by being detached from himself and constantly admonishing himself to rise above matter. What does this mean if not union with the Spirit?

Such is religion. View it as effort, apart from joy, and you will be in the wake of the preachers of all kinds who have succeeded in making it hateful while making God formidable. Fail to realize that its full joy cannot be had without separation from what is inferior in us, and your quietism will be its own punishment. In their hearts all men know this. Deep in us a true view of religion subsists intact.

CHAPTER V

Institutional Religions

INSTITUTIONAL religions are handled roughly now-a-days. Their origins are criticized, often none too sympathetically, and their impending end is joyfully announced as a matter of course. Where they refuse to modify themselves suicidal obstinacy is denounced; where they drop accessories they are mocked for giving in to exterior pressure. Unlike the King of England they can only do wrong.

Yet, as long as men are religiously-minded, they will be brought together by the similarity of their inclinations, and this will not be done without an invigorating sense of co-operation. Community will always express itself in formulas and in rites, no matter how simplified. Men will rejoice in feeling together the power of certain words, as Christians know each other by the mysterious power which some phrases in the johannine vocabulary undoubtedly possess for them. Why object to such a natural inclination? Why triumph meanly when it occasionally swerves from its path and shows human weakness instead of the divine stability? Why point out divergencies, as if they mattered more than fundamental unity?

Under the diversity of religions, purer here, more adulterated there, is religion, that is to say, God.

Where there is the highest notion of God, the greatest chances for union with Him, there religion is at its best, but it must be religion and not the semblance of it.

Apologists have done more harm than good by repeating about certain historical characters and their development, the stereotyped statement: "He, or she, unfortunately remained satisfied with a cold Theism". One may, one should, regret, that a man of Kant's type, for instance, should have been content with a too purely intellectual religion, but Theism should not be confused with the disdainful deism of Toland, Bolingbroke, or the Voltairians. Theism may be cold if it is primarily intellectual, but it can hardly be conceived as stopping at that stage. The Mystics are attracted by what many people would call mere theological entities, yet they know how to surround them with an indescribable glow.

Once more we find ourselves facing a double conception of God: one showing us the Supreme Being aloof, inaccessible and formidable; the other—endlessly alluded to in these pages—that of men and women unable to welcome the revelation of the Spirit without a feeling of passionate reverence.

Surely the Theism of Christ was not cold, and the hymns to the Holy Spirit which lend such tenderness to the Pentecostal liturgy are nothing if they are not songs of love. Why then should believers occasionally speak so lightly of the one religious belief without which none of the great religions could have any foundation?

CONCLUSION

The main ideas underlying this Part Three are, first, that there is infinitely more joy than effort in living on the higher level, and second, that, such being the case, any methods likely to introduce the notion of painful effort where attraction should suffice are unhealthy and should be corrected by simplicity, directness and sanity. Moral ideals are the natural blossoms of human development.

The immediate corollary is that we should gladly welcome the revelation of such ideals without which we should not know what is so often alluded to, nowa-days, as human dignity. Another consequence is that, when we are conscious of the juxtaposition in ourselves of that revelation and of impotency either to obtain it, unaided, or to act up to it, we should be grateful to the Superior Being to whom we owe it. Religion is the manifestation of that gratitude and should be constantly warmed up by its presence. Throw any shadow on either the propensities which make up our nobler life or on the religious sentiment accompanying them, and you destroy pure light and pure love.

If you read these lines as perhaps you read the preceding chapters, with a vague fear that they are unduly optimistic, go back to the history of philosophy or to the history of religion: you will find that they speak the same language. The narrow discouraging view of our relations with the Ideal merely belongs to the history of prejudice or misconception.

EPILOGUE

What should the effect of this book be on its readers? Encouraging, I hope. It is the work of a man who knows only too well that he lives on the plain, but keeps his window open towards the line of hills where every now and then he hears the East wind singing of another world. The idea of more light, more beauty, more love, possesses an irresistible magic: the moment we hear of people who command a wider range than ours, enjoy rarer things, and feel ready for nobler efforts, we want to be in their company, and the mere wish changes our whole outlook.

Simultaneously, we become more conscious of the everlasting hope walking beside us and whispering its questions in our ear: Am I happy? How long is my happiness going to last? Am I doing all I can to be as happy as I can? What is happiness? The more we read or think about the higher life, the more definite our personal answers to those questions will become, and the nearer we shall feel to the enjoyment of the happiness possible for us.

But this consciousness is accompanied by another which most of us know only too well, and which the psychoanalyst constantly detects, under all sorts of disguises, in men and women who profess to be free from it: that is the dread of the interruption of happiness by Death. The two images are so close to each other that frequently it takes some examination to find out which, for the time being, is leading the other. Nine men in ten, repeating what they have heard other people say, would deny that their hope of happiness was interfered with by the consideration of Death, but nine times out of ten they would be found to be inadequate readers of their own souls.

You certainly notice the tremendous effort which our modern world makes to get rid of the obsession of death, or of the horror of death which is still draping all our world in black. Medievalism felt such a terror of death that it plunged headlong into it and tried to exorcise its hideousness by desperate expression. The *danses macabres* leave no doubt about their deeper inspiration. Imagine also the disgust which, during several centuries, must have prompted people in England and France to call churchyards by such loathsome names as charnel-houses or *charniers*. Even Bossuet might clothe Death in the magnificence of seventeenth century language, but Death was to him, and appeared at his own bed-side, as the King of Terrors.

A reaction against the materialism of Death representations was necessary. It is a surprise to me that the inspiration for it should not have been found in the Christian Catacombs which seemed to be rediscovered precisely when that inspiration was needed. Whatever may be said about tradition and development, nobody will be ready to deny that the spirit of early Christianity was more transparently Christian than it has become after a long succession of ages. Now, nothing can speak of death with more tender faith or hopeful trust than do the inscriptions and the simple art of the Catacombs. There, the allusions to sleep or rest, *obdormivit, requiescit, in pace,* recover all their meaning and create an atmosphere of peace which no imagination can disturb.

Why do we prefer to that a pagan effort in which even its most ardent protagonists do not quite believe? Funeral parlors and burial-parks beautified with all sorts of pretty names inevitably recall the painted and bejewelled dead of Spain, and we know it. In the last analysis the best that light-mindedness can do to forget death is to forget its dead, a desperate course, which like all exaggerations defeats its own object. For death is like our own shadow: black-edged letters will daily come to us; the burial-park may be miles away but the clinic is round the corner, and bland physicians are as formidable as undertakers.

We may think we have definitely banished all funereal associations, but, as I said above, seldom do we rise to the exhilaration of conscious and well-grasped happiness without the sudden dread that the stroke of the clock may bring it to an end, and the simultaneous fear that another stroke of the clock must sooner or later, bring our own life to its end.

The inveterate habit we have of associating pleasure with ephemeralness is the real bane of our existence and the most powerful enemy of our peace. When Montaigne, after the Ancients, says that philosophy is the learning how to die, he really means that philosophy is the removal of the fears surrounding our notion of death. Indeed, that is our test of what true philosophy is. If some page of this book, perhaps some one of its innumerable allusions to a higher conception of God, has suddenly shown us our horizon purer and bluer, that is the page, that is the sentence or half-sentence which contains the germ of our philosophy. Let us shut up the book and live with those few words until we actually live on them. We shall soon find that where we thought we were only getting advice we have in reality taken hold of a key.

Most readers, attentive to the effects of thought on their life, will promptly discover that, no matter how nervously conscious of death they may be, this consciousness cannot co-exist with three states of mind which, with a little practice, we can enter at will:

1. keen interest in truth, even of a purely intellectual character;

2. working for any of the nobler objects possible to mankind, that is to say, what this book calls collaborating with God;

3. forgetting our own interest and devoting ourselves to the welfare or happiness of others.

The worst that Death, seen apart from immortality, can do against us is to suggest that, with its arrival, our chances for improvement may finally stop. If we feel sure that at whatever time it may interrupt us we shall be in the act of improving such chances, the terror of its visit will only be a child's bugbear of so little consequence that it will be forgotten.

The conquest of fear is no small beginning of happiness, for we have a clear notion of at least contentment, and we know it cannot exist with annoyances or paralyzing influences. However the happiness we want is superior to the rather negative condition which we call contentment. Vague though we may be about its object, we are clear about two qualities which we invariably include in its idea: we want it to possess both permanence and fulness.

The hope for permanence is a fallacy created in our mind by the deficiency of our memory. We feel sure we remember whole periods during which we were uninterruptedly happy, and that recollection creates a longing for the repetition of such periods. As a matter of fact they never existed except in our deceitful memory. There have been a few relatively undisturbed spells in our life into which happy moments seem to have been crowded. We were, in Autumn, in some beautifully sequestered mountainous region, the peace and beauty of the landscape appealed to us, our thoughts were rich and bright, people with whom we are in sympathy were near with warm appreciation whenever we wished for it. We now imagine that every minute of those periods was a climax. In reality the climaxes were, as usual, rare; it is only our imagination that multiplies them and transmutes contentment of an exceptional order into happiness.

Here we touch the other idea entering into our

notion of happiness, viz., fulness, or the presence and appreciation of the peaks of enjoyment just mentioned. Those peaks undoubtedly exist and are not mere creations of our desires. Even the most wretched mortals occasionally experience them. It goes without saying that no man can resist the passionate longing to see them revived. It is equally certain that it takes exceptional wisdom not to wish them revived in chaplets of impossibly endless joys. There lies the danger of a vague notion of happiness made even more inaccurate by the violence of our desires.

For what are the joys or climaxes we want? We do not know. Any will do if they are full enough to recall those we remember and live by. The reason is that we are seldom entirely satisfied with actualities somehow never found in pure nuggets. It is only after a time that we forget what has detracted from their perfection. Consequently the happiness we dream of is patterned after moments we do not remember quite accurately, projected into the vagueness of the unborn future. Hence the indefiniteness of our vision and the depth of the desire constantly interfering with it.

Can nothing be done to secure happiness?

Most moralists say: do not think of happiness, do not seek it, do not analyze it. A man loves his friend the better if he does not know why he loves him, and the danger of success is that by making the successful man too conscious of his goal it diminishes his chances for happiness. As Michelangelo says in one of his Sonnets:

Often I wept obtaining what I wished.

All that is true. Yet we cannot help observing that while your Stoic or pragmatist tells you to look away from happiness he adds in a whisper: if you do so, you will be happy. The conclusion must be that even the wisest are at one about happiness, regard it as the universal motive of all our actions, and only differ about the means of attaining to it. Another conclusion must be that it would be foolish to leave the satisfaction of such an elemental craving to chance, and something must be done to ensure that satisfaction.

What?

If you read the philosophers and check off what they advise by your own experience, you will find that they are agreed about the following method:

1. Forget mere desires, as you say good-bye to vague hopes of improvement, and begin at once. Begin to do what? To act. Kant says: "The greatest happiness is in store in the greatest action", and Aristotle: "Every person finds the happiness which is possible for him to attain in the act of living according to his reflection and temperate nature."

Vague? No, what we should do is what answers the best to what nature has fitted us for: thought, art, practical matters, what we do the best and with the minimum effort. The supreme act is intellection and it is rewarded by bliss, but no action is without the light which makes it rational. So act, and never cease to act. I believe that, in spite of a standardized ideal, Americans secure more average happiness than the rest of mankind because of their activity. Only each action should be accomplished with all the perfection of which its nature admits, and should be accomplished lovingly. This, of course, excludes selfishness. If the world should come to the catastrophic end, so tellingly described by Horace, and mountains should be tumbling upon one another, fearlessness would not be enough; the best would still be to do something for somebody else, and do it to the best of one's ability.

2. We should be careful to live on the highest plane possible to us. There is no other way of giving each separate action the best chance of being the noblest we are capable of. It does not require much effort to know where and when we produce our best, and where and when we are satisfied with our insignificant. There is no more difficulty in being sure about that than there is about the altitude at which our home is standing, or about the quality of the air we breathe. If we feel no doubt about the purity of our motives, the perfection of our acts will take care of itself and we shall live fully.

You recognize, I hope, the doctrine underlying every page of this book. It purports to be a plain guide to our self-perfecting but it is in reality a manual of happy living. All books dealing with self-improvement, personality, achievement, even the lower kind of achievement called success, are that: text-books of the art of being happy.

But our happiness is within us: all we need is to find its source and let it flow freely.

VITA

In his romance, *Sanguis Martyrum,* so excruciatingly touching in parts that one hardly dares to read it over again, Louis Bertrand has depicted the life which, during the second and third centuries after Christ, the Roman convicts led in the Numidian mines.

After rowing, under the whip, the galleys which conveyed their misery from every part of the Empire to Africa, they dragged their chains in long processions through the scorching rocky valleys till such of them as survived the hardships of the road finally reached Sigus.

There, they were branded on the brow with the red-hot iron, their chains were shortened so that they could not stand quite upright, not infrequently one of their eyes was gouged out, and then they were given a mallet and a lamp and disappeared under ground. Many of them were thieves or murderers, but there were also political prisoners, and there was no lack of "Atheists"—as the Christian captives were called—to whom this promiscuousness was the worst torture.

Watched by merciless foremen whose delight was to become executioners, they worked, ate, and slept in the fulsome atmosphere, or in the icy-cold dampness, of the galleries. The prefect of the mines was constantly on his guard against possible mutinies, and not the least horror in those prisoners' existence was the consciousness that they were spied upon and could hardly trust a friend. There was no hope. *Damnatus ad metalla,* sentenced to the mines, really meant sentenced to slow death in the mines. Many convicts promptly caught one of the fatal infections inevitable in such surroundings. Their bodies were hauled up a special shaft which the jargon of the prisoners dignified with a mock designation, and this was called their *apotheosis*. Some men lived to old age, gradually losing the human shape, and often sinking into brutishness before their poor souls were finally released. The whole Roman world knew of these *metalla* and spoke of them with bated breath. No death-in-life ever deserved its name so well as hard labor in the mines of Spain or Africa.

Yet, some at least of the Christians immured there managed to retain faith enough whereby to live. Here and there, on the smoother rocks, pathetic inscriptions in charcoal revealed their presence. Some of them humbly prayed for the sympathy of fellow-believers: *Holy souls, remember poor Marcianus.* Others recalled a broken affection with the hope of eternal life: *Lucilla, my sweet, thou wilt live in God for ever.* But the most frequent inscription, reiterated, as it were, in a frenzy of hope, was the repetition of a word which it required an abyss of faith to use in such an inferno. "Life" was that word, and *Vita, Vita, Vita* in long black lines, seemed like a flight of swallows chasing one another toward the light which the poor scribbler knew was shining up above. Yet, *vita* had no reference to freedom, home or love; it simply meant that the secret of the Christians was life-giving to such an extent that it must break forth in exultation.

Where we live or how we live is of little consequence. What is all-important is to *live*. The secret of the Christians is only hinted at in this book, but the revelation of the Spirit fills it. Enough for us at least to whisper in gratitude *Vita, Vita!* And if we ponder those talismanic words, soon they will swell to a song, and our every day will be transformed by their magic.

INDEX